This book is dedicated to my son Daniel, my forever hero.

The angel appeared to him and said,
"Mighty hero, the Lord is with you!" Judges 6:12

Love
Is In the
Journey

A YOUNG BOY'S STRUGGLES TO SURVIVE
ADVERSITY AFTER A LIFE CHANGING TRAUMA

*Love never gives up, never loses faith is always hopeful,
and endures through every circumstance. (1 Corinthians 13:7)*

DANIELLE AUGUSTINE

BALBOA.
PRESS

A DIVISION OF HAY HOUSE

Balboa Press books may be ordered through booksellers or by contacting:

Balboa Press
A Division of Hay House
1663 Liberty Drive
Bloomington, IN 47403
www.balboapress.com
1 (877) 407-4847

Because of the dynamic nature of the Internet, any web addresses or links contained in this book may have changed since publication and may no longer be valid. The views expressed in this work are solely those of the author and do not necessarily reflect the views of the publisher, and the publisher hereby disclaims any responsibility for them.

The author of this book does not dispense medical advice or prescribe the use of any technique as a form of treatment for physical, emotional, or medical problems without the advice of a physician, either directly or indirectly. The intent of the author is only to offer information of a general nature to help you in your quest for emotional and spiritual well-being. In the event you use any of the information in this book for yourself, which is your constitutional right, the author and the publisher assume no responsibility for your actions.

Any people depicted in stock imagery provided by Thinkstock are models, and such images are being used for illustrative purposes only.
Certain stock imagery © Thinkstock.

Interior Graphics/Art Credit: Shutterstock

Print information available on the last page.

ISBN: 978-1-5043-6946-6 (sc)
ISBN: 978-1-5043-6945-9 (hc)
ISBN: 978-1-5043-6947-3 (e)

Library of Congress Control Number: 2016918312

Balboa Press rev. date: 05/25/2017

Contents

Together

For the times in your life

You are feeling alone

Take hold of my hand

And I will bring you back home

Acknowledgments

To my son, Daniel. You have been and still are my strength, courage, support system, and most of all, my passion to move forward in writing this story. Your love and loyalty has made me a changed woman. My years with you were the greatest times in my life, although you have faced so much adversity, obstacles, and challenges. I am honored we did this journey together, as a team. I love you more than life, and I am privileged to be your mother. How you ever put up with me, I can only sum it up to be trust and unconditional love. Your love has forever set me free.

To my husband, TJ. You always told me no matter how tough things have become or will become, I should never give up and should pick my battles wisely. Thank you for the years of putting up with me while I was bucking the system to keep our son safe. He was my first priority while I was repeatedly being kicked down picking myself up again and again. I promise you that I will not give up. I will prevail.

To my daughter, Laura, who needs a halo over her head just alone for putting up with me through all her growing years. Thank you for all the sacrifices you made on your brother's behalf, when you had so many of your own family challenges to deal with—and boy, were they challenges. You are a gift of a daughter, mother, sister, and friend to all you touch. Anyone would be proud and privileged to have you in their life. Your brother loves you so much. Always carry that with you in your caring heart. Also, thank you for helping me with this book, I could not have done it without you. I have tortured you on a daily basis to put this mess of a manuscript together—and you did so while working, raising four children on your own, and finishing your bachelor's degree in nursing. Now on to the master's! I am so proud of all the accomplishments you have achieved in your life, and the best one was being your brother's lifeline when he needed you. I love you forever.

To my four grandchildren, Daniel, Matthew, Krista, and Ryan, for putting up with my constant complaining when it was I you should be complaining about. Sorry for laying so many things on you all. Always know I will be there for you, and I love you for your patience, understanding, commitment, and love. You are my heroes and have been such an inspiration to me.

To my best childhood friend, Carole, whom I love more than anything in the world. You stood by me in my darkest hours when I was growing up through some very tough times. You were my rock. When you told me you were gay at a young age and I was straight, it was at that moment we established a bond, and I knew then we were friends till the end. Our bond will never be broken. Please know I will always be there for you. You are my hero, and for that I love you forever.

To my best adulthood friend, Jean, who passed in 2010. When we connected in our middle thirties, I knew I had a big challenge on my hands. You were headstrong much like myself. We butted heads quite often, but as time passed our connection was obvious. We were going to be bonded friends forever. You were always there for me, my family and mostly Daniel. You brought so much light to all of us. Till we meet again my dear friend. Love forever.

To Paula, Mom #2, for all the times you shared with Daniel, and for your commitment to him in his time of need. For the days and hours you spent sacrificing out of love and devotion for him. They say true commitment comes out of love, and you certainly fit the bill. Although we had our differences, your love for him was not one of them. You were a rock for him and shared great times together. In his eyes and heart, you earned the title of Mom #2. No matter what happens, that will never be forgotten.

To Daniel's best girlfriend ever, Carissa, for being the rock, the mountain, and the pinnacle of what a caring human being is all about. In sickness or in health, you were there for both when he needed you. Even with your own disability, you never missed an appointment for him when he needed to go to NYC. You came by bus with your own health aid to New Jersey to spend days at a time with him. We all had so much fun, especially Daniel; he loves being with you. You are someone we are so proud of, and you are a part of our family. You are like a daughter to me and will forever remain in my heart. You are truly a strong, smart, intelligent woman who weathered many storms in life with your own disability, and you fought them all with such grace. Never forget how much we love you and your beautiful spirit.

To Debbie, for being there for Laura and me when we needed you. You were the one who reconnected me to my son when I was at the worst time of my life. If it wasn't for that experience, I might not be here today. I don't think you realize what an important part you played in how I now live my life. Friends like you are forever, and you're a true friend.

To Daniel's best bus driver, Iris, for taking him safely to his Friday night fun program, but also for being a loving and loyal friend. He loves you so much. You will forever be in his heart.

To Steve, Thank you for all the memorabilia you gave to Daniel for his Pepsi collection. This made him very happy, your generosity will always be remembered.

To my favorite talk show host, Dr. Phil, for giving me the needed advice to write this book on my own. Yes, family does come first. Your compassion for people's lives especially our most vulnerable children was enough for me to know that at seventy years old, it is still not too late to have my voice heard. Thank you.

To Dr. Charles Stanley. Thank you for your Sunday sermons, which give me so much hope and comfort. You are an inspiration to me. God bless you.

To Dr. David Jeremiah. Thank you for your Sunday sermons, which have lifted my spirit with hope and given me much wisdom about God and the Bible. God bless you.

To Joel Osteen. Thank you for giving the world hope through your ministry. God bless you.

To Dr. Wayne Dyer. At the very end of my writing this book, I was very fortunate to have been able to make a connection with this Hay House author, who passed on August 20, 2015. I was encouraged by his love and passion for mankind. Thank you for the gift of my being able to continue on with my writing through yours. I look forward to learning many more lessons about life's love and commitment.

To Marsha Manion, publishing consultant. Thank you for your kindness and respect in my travels on this book journey. I want to thank you for making the turmoil-filled experience of putting this book together somewhat bearable for me and my family. Most of all, Daniel thanks you.

To Nicole Tarrega, publishing services associate and the design team. Thank you for your patience and understanding in making my vision for this book come to life for me and Daniel.

To God and Lord Jesus for guiding me back to church, the Bible, and scripture.

All scriptures in this book were taken from the Hard Cover Holy Bible, New Living Translation 1996, 2004, 2007. ISBN-978-1-4143-1430-3

Introduction

WHAT I BELIEVED to be my conception of the justice system from my childhood to my adulthood was a lesson to be learned not only for myself but for my entire family. I believed the system was to be there for families in their times of need, but it was a far cry from the reality. There are too many victims of many different crimes: murder, greed, elder abuse, disabled abuse, and child abuse. It is these poor defenseless victims who suffer most, not the criminals.

The real lesson to be learned is how well we deal with the challenges and obstacles that cross our path, and how we allow them to affect our lives. They can be looked at as negative, or we can take the bull by the horns and move forward in a positive way, refusing to allow the persons involved to walk away without punishment or consequences; we can receive justice for our loved ones. I wish I could say my experiences that involved my son's life in the system were all positive, but they were not. The truth is, it was hell and back with much pain and suffering and a tremendous amount of grief.

> *My suffering was good for me, for it taught me to pay attention*
> *to your degrees, your instructions were more valuable to me*
> *than millions in gold and silver. (Psalm 119:71–72)*

Many times through my life, I asked myself, "Why do bad things happen to good people?" I still have no answer. The reality is there is no answer, at least not the one I am looking for. I wrote this book as a way to reach out to the many families who have children in the system with mental and physical disabilities. They need to move forward no matter how hard the system tries to buck them. They must not fail their loved ones, who are exposed and victimized by the very system that is there to protect them. They need to be a major part of the fight to protect our disabled. This is why I needed to write this book: our love ones need our voices! When the system knows you are fighting for the rights of your loved ones, it will keep them on alert. Remember that strength comes in numbers. I must defend my son and continue on my commitment to not let him down.

> *"I will make you into a great nation. I will bless you and make you famous, and you will be a blessing to others. I will bless those who bless you and curse those who treat you with contempt. All the families on earth will be blessed through you." (Genesis 12:2-3)*

> *A letter from Paul, Dear brothers and sisters, We can't help but thank God for you, because your faith is flourishing and your love for one another is growing. We proudly tell God's other churches about your endurance and faithfulness in all the persecutions and hardships you are suffering. And God will use this persecution to show his justice and to make you worthy of his kingdom, for which you are suffering. In his justice he will payback those who persecute you. (2 Thessalonians (1: 3, 4, 5-6)*

While I was writing, I was at a standstill. I had loss of energy and no direction. I needed to stop feeling defeated. My son never wanted me to give up fighting a system that I tried so hard to go up against so many times. I did not raise my son his whole life, and watch him go through so much, to wind up having the system defeat him. I pray every day to God to help me move on with my writing. He answers me by my being able to pick up a pen and continue on. To Daniel, the system became his disability. These bad apples hindered my son by hiding behind the desks from which they made their speeches, earned their money, and told their lies.

This book is not a book about hate or revenge. It is a story about the reality of a fallen system. Here is a glimpse into some events that led to my family being involved with the system and the many challenges and obstacles we have experienced on this journey. My wish is to have my son's story appreciated, and hopefully it will have an impact.

> *Show me the right path, Oh Lord; Point out the road for me to follow. Lead me by your truth and teach me, for you are the God who saves me. All day long I put my hope in you. (Psalm 25:4- 5)*

> *Pilate said, "So you are a king? "Jesus responded, "You say I am a King. Actually, I was born and came into this world to testify to the truth. All who love the truth recognize that what I say is true."(John 18:37)*

Chapter 1

The Beginning

MY LIFE WAS far from uneventful. I hit many tough spots while growing up, but somehow I always managed to pull through. I was the youngest of eleven children, six sisters and four brothers. My firstborn brother passed away from blood poisoning at twelve weeks old due to an unclean instrument used during circumcision. I remember growing up and watching my mom every May 29 mourn the loss of her firstborn son. She would go about her day doing all her chores, I could feel her pain and loss, but it was not until I grew up and went on to have my own children that I truly connected with her grief.

My father passed on at age fifty-one from cancer, when I was nine years old. The bubble I was living in as a child was broken, and life before would never be the same again. His passing for me meant much loss, pain, and confusion. The days after his passing, I began forming a shell for my own protection. I no longer had the love and security he gave to me when he was alive; I felt deserted by his death. My father was my world, and he always looked out for me, especially when I was around many of my much older siblings, who did not have time for me because they were married and had their own families. I was considered Daddy's little girl. Although I liked the attention he showed me, I was no {Prima Donna!}

One of my older brothers was married to a great wife whom he met while he was in the navy. He had three children, and they moved to Long Island so he could build homes. With my father now gone, my big brother decided to take over his role as head of household. Big mistake! This is when things started to change for the worst. My father was the one who enforced the rules. Although he was a great role model, he had his own standards for raising his children with some degree of discipline—but not where abuse was any part of it. As the youngest, I always felt protected by my father. That was about to change!

After Dad's passing, Mom became distraught, which was understandable. My oldest sister and her daughter lived with us. They moved in after my sister had a nervous breakdown due to the breakup of her marriage. I didn't mind because my niece was the same age as me; we were like sisters. My brother Frankie was also still living at home. Frankie was mildly, mentally disabled. Do to his disability he had a very special relationship with Mom. Oh, how he adored her! The problem was now Mom was getting older and dealing with a headstrong nine-year-old girl. Big brother would come in for visits and to check on things. Mom started occasionally shipping me off to my brother's home in Long Island. He would approach me and stick his finger in my face while telling me to walk the straight line in his infamous harsh tone that we were accustomed to by now.

Without Dad around, life was different. I usually went to my best friend Carol's house whenever my brother came over in order to stay out of his way and avoid his wrath. I spent many hours with her mother and father, and I felt very safe there. My other siblings knew of his behavior, and so did Mom. They were aware of his outbursts of anger toward me and his wife, but there were no repercussions. What it boiled down to was that no one in my family at the time was willing to step up to the plate and confront him. Most of the time I fended for myself. My brother was like a caged animal let out to roam after Dad's passing.

Time passed, and I survived my young childhood until my teens. I kept myself in survival mode, and was always on guard when it came to big brother. My brother was still coming to the house, but I was older now and was able to avoid many of his visits. I was fortunate but not out of the woods. I was not always able to escape the abuse of my brother. His physical choice of abuse was to choke me, resulting in me passing out. There was no sexual abuse involved. Mom knew about it but did not do anything to stop him, So many times I felt my days were numbered; I did not believe I was going to make it to my eighteenth birthday. I had always had that number in my head, and I believed if I passed it, I would be safe and out of his sadistic clutches. My goal was to save myself. I guess that was my safety net back then, holding on to hope so I could keep up my survival mode without giving up.

> Be strong and courageous, all you who put hope in the Lord!
> (Psalm 31:24)

At the age of fifteen, I went to my neighborhood police station and begged them to lock me up so Big Brother couldn't get to me. I explained to them what my brother was doing to me during his visits. They reached out to him, gave him a strict warning, and sent me home. I begged them to keep me at the station, but the police assured me I was going to be okay. I was resentful for their lack of securing my safety when I was so fearful of my brother. They were the ones who were supposed to be there to protect me. The police station was six blocks from my home, and the captain lived right around the corner. All that protection around me, and yet I was still in harm's way. Figure that one out! For me, that was the start of the system failing.

Things were quiet for a few weeks. Then Big Brother came to visit Mom, and I was on guard for him to go off about my visit to the police station. Sure enough, he walked in and showed his wrath, yelling directly at me and saying, "Were you a good girl today?" This time it was different.

My older sister was at the table sewing clothes. By now she developed into a tough cookie. She jumped up from the table holding a pair of scissors in her hand and told him to leave me alone, or else she was going to hurt him. She told him he should pay the consequences for his past behavior toward me, and he should never touch me again. From that day forward, Big Brother backed off, and my sister became my hero. Although grateful, I was still afraid of him, and I was going to stay in survival mode until my eighteenth birthday. I believed if I reached this goal, it would be a great achievement. Growing up into my adulthood, I had issues resulting from my brother's abuse. This left me with an eating and swallowing disorder. I also had severe anxiety that led me to using paper bags and an inhaler to breathe due to a lack of oxygen. Fortunately, I was able to address these issues by seeking medical care and counseling to cope.

> *I was living quietly until he shattered me. He took me by the neck and broke me in pieces. Then he set me up as his target, and now his archers surround me. (Job 16:12-13)*

> *I love you, Lord, you are my strength. The Lord is my rock, my fortress, and my savior, my God is my rock, in whom I find protection. He is my shield, the power that saves me, and my place of safety. I called on the Lord, who is worthy of praise, and he saved me from my enemies. (Psalm 18:1-2-3)*

Chapter 2

My First Love

....

IT WAS 1964 when I met the love of my life. He was twenty-four, and I was seventeen. I enjoyed spending many of my summers going to my favorite theme park, Coney Island. I loved the rides and the freedom of going to the nearby beach with my friends. There was an arcade near the park, and I often hung around there. This was where my first love and I met. He was quite handsome with black hair and beautiful deep brown eyes. It was love at first sight for the both of us. When my siblings found out about our relationship, they were not happy about it because he was older than me and of Spanish descent, but I continued to see him anyway. It wasn't long after that I found out I was pregnant.

My love was previously married with no children. He and his ex-wife had parted ways; she was a very mature and refined lady, a class act. She had much more than I had going for me back then. They say wisdom comes with age, and she had plenty of that. I was younger, and our age difference showed that. When I reflect back on my past encounters with the ex-wife, she was rooting for me. She was not able to have children of her own, so when she found out I was pregnant, she was actually happy for me. That is what being a caring person is about. She loved her ex-husband enough to wish him the best. She told me to move on with my life and take good care of my child when she or he was born. The short time we connected was a powerful experience, and I will never forget it. God bless her, wherever she is.

I moved out of my home for a short time and found an apartment down the block from my mom's house with reasonable rent. I was going to move in with my baby's father because the pressure put on me from my family about my pregnancy, and them alienating me from the love of my life, was too much. He was so happy we were going to be together, but that did not last long. After several months, I made the decision to move back home with my mom and brother Frankie. Mom was not feeling well, and the pressure was on me to take care of her despite being pregnant. My love was very upset I was going back home, but I felt guilty about Mom being ill.

As the months passed, my pregnancy was progressing. My second oldest brother was voicing some very hurtful remarks to me for having my baby out of wedlock. The pressure of staying home became too much for me; I was always under their thumb. This time Mom stepped up to the plate, unlike when I was being abused by Big Brother. She told me when I was alone with her one day not to feel bad because my brother also had a child out of wedlock. Talk about the pot calling the kettle black!

Chapter 3

The Arrival of My Baby Boy

AT EIGHTEEN I gave birth to a son, whom I named Daniel. What a beautiful gift! He was seven pounds, five ounces of pure love and joy. I was thankful to God for pulling me through. My family was still not happy with me having a child with my love. Back in the 1960s, there were people who had their opinions and prejudices, and unfortunately it is still going on today. My best friend Carole being gay knew all about these people, and not having their stamp of approval.

After my son's birth, I was going through hard times following the decision I had made: my son was to have no contact with his father because of my family's negative feelings against him and alienation toward me. After staying home for many months, Mom convinced me to go out with my friends while she stayed home and watched Daniel; she said I needed some downtime. I realized she felt bad for me being so confused and unhappy. I was lonely and still in love with my son's father. I know one thing for sure: one day when the time came for me to leave this earth, I would have known what true love between a man, a woman, and a child was all about. I was so gifted to have been able to experience this magical time in my life. What a beautiful thought to take with me on the day I take my final breath on this earth.

Daniel's father and I drifted apart from my own regretful decisions I made due to my siblings' continual interference in my life. To this day, I still carry my first love close to my heart, and he will forever be my soul mate and a part of the creation of my precious son.

Not long after I started going out, I met a man my age, nineteen. Ironically, he had the same name as my son's father. I continued to see him; I guess it would be called dating, but I called it hanging out. Mom approved of him, and so did the family because he seemed like the all-American boy. Everything seemed good, but the problem was I did not love him. I continued to see him and took my family's advice to marry him when my son was seven months old. He had a large family of sisters and brothers, and they were opposed to him marrying me with a child. I think back to that time and reflect on all their hurtful remarks. I would ask, "Why would anyone want to stop someone from raising an innocent child?" I guess they had prejudice against my son, just as my family did for Daniel's father. They looked at their brother like he was above me and my son, because he and his brothers came from a family of iron workers, who were looked upon as the elite back in those days. They believed my son and I were not good enough for him. I truly felt more pity for them than anger. Daniel was an innocent human being. These people did not deserve to share in his life. SHAME, SHAME, on them all.

> *Are we all not children of the same father? Are we not created by the same God? Then why do we betray each other violating the convent of our ancestors? (Malachi 2:10)*

> *Then he says to them, anyone who welcomes a little child like this on my behalf★ welcomes me, and anyone who welcomes me also welcomes my father who sent me. Whoever is the least among you is the greatest. (Luke 9:48)*

Several years into my marriage, I reconnected with Daniel's father. I was not in love with my husband. It was not long into my marriage before I found out he had a gambling and drinking problem. It became clear to me that before I married him, there were many skeletons hidden in his family's closets. All of his four brothers also had gambling and drinking addictions. The people in the glass houses always seem to be the ones who throw the stones. I believed at that time I was justified to reconnect with my son's father because of the farce of a marriage I was in. It turned out my son would pay the price for that decision. Daniel was reaching his third birthday, and I was fully aware I married for all the wrong reasons. I thought he could give me a good life and didn't realize he carried so much baggage. Mr. Right turned out to be Mr. Wrong, and I wanted out at any cost.

> *"That is the whole story here now is my final conclusion,"*
> *fear God and obey his commands for that is everyone's duty.*
> *God will judge us for everything we do including every secret*
> *thing we do good or bad. (Ecclesiastes 12:13–14)*

As the marriage continued, my mother regretted having given me input on marrying him. Mom witnessed how unhappy I was by his actions whenever he was in her company. She wanted love and happiness for Daniel and I, and this man was never going to fit the bill. All I needed was to be back with my first love, whom I missed so much.

Chapter 4

The Accident

IT WAS TUESDAY, June 7, 1968. This was the day Daniel's and my world fell apart. It was an unusually hot day. I was going to meet my son's father, and we were going to reunite. Happily ever after, I thought. I had planned it for many months. We were both excited to finally be able to come together again after so much heartache in our lives. I thought it was meant to be, and we would reconnect our love again.

I had already packed my bags and had written my husband a letter—I guess one would call it a Dear John letter. I was not overly concerned because it was a chance for me and my son to discover the real love and happiness we deserved. I hoped my husband would find the help he needed for his gambling addiction. If he didn't, he was never going to live a fruitful life as long as he carried his demons around that also included carousing with women. I had witnessed this behavior for two and a half years, and I resented him for it. I certainly did not sign up for it. My husband went off to his job that morning, and I had made plans to take my son to the local park; I had promised him we would have lunch there. I would then still have time to go home, grab my bags, and go. A few weeks prior to that day, Mom was released from the hospital, and my sisters and I were taking turns to help her out. This day in June was not my turn. All I wanted was to fulfill my son's wishes to go to the park and run in the sprinklers. I wanted to return home early enough to avoid any confrontation before my husband returned from work. I left my apartment and had about nine blocks to walk.

As I was approaching the park around 11:00 a.m., my sister was exiting her car on her way to approach me. Today was her day to help with Mom. She told me something had come up, and she could not do it. I felt my plans were more important than her issue. She pleaded with me again. I explained my promise to Daniel, but she continue to plead. As annoyed and agitated as I felt, she insisted I was her only hope. At this time I was also aware my other sister was usually in the park with her children. I figured I would take a quick look and ask her if she would watch Daniel and keep a sharp eye on him in his carriage while I ran to Mom's. Daniel was a very energetic toddler, so I gave my sister strict orders to not let him out of his carriage. He was very comfortable where he was and had a canopy over him to give him shade.

I went to Mom's apartment, about fifteen blocks from the park. I was to help her get washed, dressed, take her to the beauty salon and then pick her up in one hour to take her home. After I dropped off Mom, I was walking back to the park to spend time with my son while she had her hair done. I was approaching the park and walked over to where Daniel was sitting in his carriage, waiting for me to take him out. I could see he looked quite overheated. His blond hair was stuck to his tiny face, and he was all red. At that moment I felt so guilty seeing all of the other children playing just feet away. I was overwhelmed with all different emotions. I was so angry that I made the decision to go to my mother's. I was the youngest and always had to be the one to step up to the plate. Although I had told her not to let Daniel out of the carriage I did not intend for her to leave him there overheated without even attempting to cool him down. In the 1960s, we did not have cell phones to communicate, so I could not call my sister to see how my son was doing and to check whether he was drinking enough fluids to keep him cool and hydrated. I reached into the carriage and released my son from the harness. I lifted him out and pointed him toward the sprinklers with his clothes on so he could get some instant relief from the heat. I turned around and focused on my sister for a few seconds and verbally lashed out at her.

When I turned back around, Daniel was gone. I frantically searched for my boy at the sprinkler. Behind the wall of the sprinkler, my eyes zoomed everywhere. I panicked and looked toward the entrance of the park. There was a group of people standing there in a circle. Out of the circle was one woman screaming, "Does anyone here have little boy with a white tee shirt, blue shorts, and white shoes?" That comment was followed by her screaming—he was struck down by a car. I can still hear her to this very day.

At that moment my whole world fell apart. I ran out of the park and across the street in the opposite direction from the entrance. I was in shock. In order to avoid what I knew was reality, I ran to a row of houses and started banging on doors, laughing and crying at the same time. I recall a young women opening her front door, and I stumbled into her living room. I believe she was in the company of an older gentleman who was her father. The woman tried to calm me down with a glass of water and a pill that I vaguely remember refusing. I was wandering around her living room not making much sense of what was happening. I remember thanking her and the man and then running out of the house. By this time the ambulance had taken Daniel to the hospital with my sister, who rode in the ambulance with him. I remember running and running; I found out later that I went home. The bags I had packed and the letter I had left for my husband were there, and it clicked what I was doing and my plans of leaving him for a better life. Now that was never going to be a reality. The reality was the family I wanted was over. I unpacked the bag, ripped up the letter, and somehow found my way to the hospital. To this day, I still do not know how I made it there. As time passed, I was able to put together many pieces, but not all of them. I simply knew my baby boy was hurt, and I was afraid of not knowing whether he was going to live or die. Nothing in the world mattered except his life.

I know the trauma of this horrific accident blocked out many unanswered questions. Why did I go to my apartment first instead of the hospital? I did not know why back then, but after years of trying to put many things together after the accident, I believe my going home was my way of protecting the family I had left. I was trying to put things back together again. In reality, I was trying to erase my prior actions of leaving. I know now it was my subconscious working to shield me from more shame and guilt. I know I left my mom in the beauty salon that day. My sister for whom I did the favor picked her up.

To this day I have never been able to shed the guilt of leaving my precious son in the playground with my sister. It never leaves you. All of the ifs and whys never leave you. It doesn't matter who tries to tell me I'm not at fault. It never goes away.

Fools make fun of guilt, but the Godly acknowledge it and seek reconciliation. The house of the wicked will be destroyed, But the tent of the Godly will flourish. (Proverbs 14:9-10-11)

After all these years, I still relive the accident every day. I ask myself the big what-if. What if I had not gone to my mother's that day? The answer is that Daniel would never have been in harm's way. What if I missed my sister on the way to the park? She would have had to ask someone else. The answers to those two questions are clear now: my son's accident would have never happened. All I have heard for years was it was not my fault. I was told I was a good mother. It was never about me being a good mother—it was about the guilt I felt that horrific day. When a parent professes to love their child, and that child becomes injured or is put in harm's way, whether the child was in your care or someone else's, you cannot help but blame yourself. I do know I never intentionally meant to hurt the most precious human being in my life, but the guilt sticks to my heart like glue and takes over the core of my soul. It became part of my makeup and lingered over my life like a dark cloud.

> *One of the serpents flew to me with a burning coal he had taken from the altar with a pair of tongs. He touched my lips with it and said, "See, this coal has touched your lips. Now your guilt is removed and your sins are forgiven." (Isaiah 6:6-7)*

Chapter 5

The Hospital

WHEN I ARRIVED at the hospital, it was early afternoon. There were nurses and doctors everywhere scrambling in the emergency room. I paced back and forth, wanting this bad nightmare to be over. I wanted the doctor to come out and tell me my baby boy was alive and was going to be okay. My husband came over to me. I do not know till this very day who informed him and never asked. It was so confusing and felt like I was having an out-of-body experience. I was there in the flesh, but my mind was not. I was somewhere else in time, floating above all the chaos and going around in circles or in a maze, and I could not find my way out. I believe I developed an instant shield to protect myself, like I had when my father passed. I was once again in survival mode.

Finally a young doctor came out asking, "Where is the boy's mom?" I yelled to him, "Here I am." He stated that my baby boy, two months away from his third birthday, had suffered severe head trauma. His skull was fractured on the left side, and his brain was swelling. He also had a broken arm and internal injuries. This hit me like a bomb exploding inside me. He then informed me Daniel needed to have brain surgery to remove the bone fragments that had scattered all over his skull in small splinters. Two brain surgeons would be operating on my son to try to save his life. The doctor stated there was a short amount of time to get my son stabilized. I literally felt dead inside, like an empty shell. All this trauma, pain, and suffering was brought upon my tiny little boy, who had never done anything wrong in his short life. All he ever wanted was to go to the playground and have fun.

The operation went on until the early morning of June 8. I wanted to see my baby boy so badly. The surgeon came out of the operating room to inform me to go with the nurse to see my boy, because they did not believe he would survive through the night. I was in shock and could not fathom what I was hearing. I wanted to scream out loud and run away. I could not focus on what he was telling me. Could all this be happening?

I went in, and it seemed like forever since I had seen my son at the playground. He was lying there, looking so innocent and vulnerable with his tiny body all bandaged. His head was so swollen, like a bowling ball. There were tubes everywhere, and he was naked because he had an extremely high temperature. Daniel was lying on a flat table. His body was blue because he was having trouble breathing. I felt like I was in a black tunnel. It was the most helpless, lonely, devastating feeling in the whole world. Yesterday I was a twenty-one-year-old mom, and Daniel was two months away from his third birthday. Now my tiny boy was struggling to survive. We had only each other. Even at his young age, he was smart beyond his years. He was so loving, funny, and caring. He was a happy boy, and now I was facing his destiny. Was my boy going to live or die?

I was allowed to spend only a very short time with him while a nurse stood by. In what seemed like a blink of an eye, another nurse rushed back in the room and stated to me that the doctor needed to see me ASAP. My body went numb. The doctor was in the corridor outside the room Daniel was in, and I stood in front of him. He informed me my son needed another operation. I shouted back, "Doctor, my son just spent the night in surgery, being operated on his brain, eleven hours and he looks so very bad. How can he withstand another surgery?" He stated he needed me to sign a permission release form for a tracheostomy. I said I could not do it—I was too afraid. The doctor informed me if I did not sign the papers for surgery, he would have to seek a court order. He stated that the time he would have to take to get a court order could cost my son his life. He said it needed to be done to allow him to breathe; that was why Daniel was so blue. I gave my signed permission to the doctor and entered the elevator to go back to the waiting room, where some of my family still waited.

> *But Jesus said, "Let the children come to me. Don't stop them! For the kingdom of heaven belongs to those who are like these children." (Matthew 19:14)*

Chapter 6

The Turnaround

A TRACHEOTOMY WAS performed, and that was the turning point of Daniel's long recovery. My son's biological father was notified of the accident. I still do not know who informed him, and I never asked; I believe it was by one of my friends. When he arrived at the hospital, I panicked because I did not want my husband to have any contact with him or to become aware of the plans I made to reunite with my son's father on the very day of the accident. This led me to make the second worst decision of my life. I asked the security guards to escort Daniel's biological father out of the hospital. It is a decision I have regretted and lived with my whole life. To this day, it is etched on my soul as one of my many regrets that changed the course of our lives.

As the weeks slowly went by, I lived by my son's side in the hospital room. I sat with him day and night, talking to him about all the things he loved to do in his short life, especially watching the Flintstones, playing with his toys, and being a comic. He loved to make people laugh and was certainly a character. There was a large window in the room, and I would often go from Daniel's bed to look out, dreaming how much I wanted us to be on the outside, where life was going on as usual. Daniel was in a coma, and the doctor continued to encourage me to talk to him and pray. He informed me that one of the things affected by his brain trauma was his hearing.

It was the first to come back when coming out of coma. Hearing my voice would hopefully enhance my son's recovery. I was asked if Daniel happened to be left-handed. He was left-handed like me. This made the doctor very pleased because it meant my son's speech had a good chance of being restored; the part of the brain that controlled speech was on the opposite side of where the trauma was.

Daniel's recovery days following the surgery were up and down. It was minute by minute. And hour by hour. My son was faced with all different challenges. He had to have his head turned to the right side for several months due to swelling of the brain. He had internal bleeding. Daniel was such a gallant fighter with every single challenge. Last rites were given to him several times by a wonderful chaplain, and I was so at peace when he came to pray.

"I have one small request to make of you, "she said. "I hope you won't turn me down." "What is it mother? He asked. "You know I won't refuse you. (1 Kings 2:20)

But God heard the boy crying, and the angel of God called to Hagar from heaven; Hagar what's wrong? Do not be afraid! God has heard the boy crying as he lies there. Go to him and comfort him for I will make a great nation from his descendants. (Genesis 21:17–18)

I was soon able to tube feed my son. The staff allowed me to do so because I hardly ever left his side. I had lost sixty pounds in two months and was down to eighty-two pounds. I could not eat food. I felt guilty when I attempted to eat. I survived on liquids and potato chips here and there. I knew I needed to keep my strength for his sake, but the guilt overtook me. One of the hardest things for me to have witnessed was my son having the tracheostomy. He had to be suctioned several times every day and night. He would choke when the tube was inserted down his trach, and he would turn blue while gasping for air. Along with this he was still recovering from his other injuries. He still had internal bleeding and broken bones. His ear was partially rubbed off when the car hit him and dragged him against the hot pavement. Watching my son suffering was hell and back and then back to hell again. He had to be put in a tent with hot moisture to prevent him from getting pneumonia.

> *Lord hear my prayer! Listen to my plea! Don't turn away from me in my time of distress. Bend down to listen. And answer me quickly when I call you. For my days disappear like smoke, and my bones burn like red - hot coals. My heart is sick, withered like grass, and I lost my appetite, Because of my groaning, I am reduced to skin and bones. (Psalm 102:1-5)*

Vincent

During Daniel's stay, there was a young boy named Vincent who had a cancerous brain tumor. Vincent was a handsome boy of twelve years old with black hair and beautiful brown eyes. He had a younger brother with blond hair and blue eyes who was around ten. They had two great parents who were of Italian decent, a very tight-knit and caring family. Vincent had a shunt in his head that was put in after the tumor was unsuccessfully removed because of the location. We shared in the pain and heartache from each other's tragedies. There was no difference because we all had to watch our children suffer, and it was debilitating. Before the family went home, we exchanged phone numbers. Although it was sad to see them leave, I was happy to see them finally go home. Away from all the chaos, heartache, and pain of the hospital drama. Now I was left to move forward with the other families with whom I had connected.

Several years later, I was sifting through my personal papers when I came across Vincent's parents' phone number. When I decided to muster up some nerve and call, I was able to reach the mom. We exchanged our hellos and pleasantries. I needed to know how Vincent was because he was always on my mind. After a short pause, his mom told me that he had passed. I was devastated. Although I was aware he had cancer, I had not understood the full impact of him being gone. I was just remembering him being so young and walking through the floor of the pediatric center looking so alive. I said I was sorry. When I hung up the phone, I was left with such sadness, but at the same time I was grateful that my son had survived his accident. Unfortunately, this was another wake-up call for me about how fragile life was. I still reflect back to Vincent often. His family and I formed a bond over a tragedy that will last forever. God bless them.

Baby Girl

When a code was called on a tiny baby girl who had a heart problem, the doctor ran in the room and asked me to hold up the plastic hood that was covering her small sleeping area, so he could work on her as soon as possible. While help was running all about to save her, I stood there the whole time staring at this beautiful soul who'd just started in life with a horrific challenge ahead. Unfortunately, she passed shortly after.

Little Boys

While Daniel was still in a coma, there was a young boy who was abused by a family member, bruised over his face and body. He had no visitors while he was there except for social services. I could not comprehend why anyone would want to hurt a small, innocent child. Another boy was being watched by his older sister while their mother was at another hospital having a hysterectomy, and he fell out of a second floor window. The mother had to leave the hospital to be with her son. She could barely walk. Unfortunately, he passed away.

Teacup Girl

There was a beautiful young Spanish girl who was two and a half years old. She had a hole in her tiny heart. She had a mother who was so loving and dedicated. The mother had bought her to the hospital on two occasions because she would turn blue. I witnessed the doctors and nurses coming in and out of the room over and over to take her blood. She was stuck with needles all day and never complained. This little champ smiled and was happy to have her mom there. She would stay from morning till evening, and then she needed to go home to her other children. I reassured her I would watch over her baby girl. In the next few days, the mom decided to take her little girl home and not have the operation that the doctors believed would save her life. She was so scared and could not bring herself to do it. Several days went by, and the mom was back again. She told me this time she would go through with the surgery. She could not see her daughter suffer any longer. The girl was so tiny and frail, and I wanted so badly for her to be okay. The mom had brought up a set of dishes, saucers, and cups for her to play with, and boy did she love them.

The evening before surgery, the mom went home late and planned on coming early the next morning before her baby's surgery. I was there every day and night, so I stayed with her baby girl. We would pass the time by playing with her little dishes, but she would cry out for her mom. I was truly heartbroken. The doctor came in very early the next day to take her to surgery. I asked why they could not wait for her mom to come. They explained to me it would be better for both mom and child to not let them connect, because it would be too hard on them both. I was against this decision but had no control over the events that were happening.

When the mom came in, her world began to unravel. She was so upset her baby girl was gone. It seemed like forever passed before the doctor came into the waiting room to inform the mom and her brother (who just came home from the army) that the operation was over and was a success. All one could hear were words of love and thanks to the doctor, along with many hugs from the mom. I was so happy for her. It was not long after that the doctor came back in again, this time to tell the mom her baby girl took a turn for the worse and had passed. God, how I cried for her and the pain she was in. It was so devastating. The hours after she passed, I stared in disbelief at the empty bed that this beautiful baby girl had once occupied. Then the nurse came in to quickly empty the nightstand, which held the girl's hairbrush and dishes. At first I was so angry, and then I was sad because I knew that was what the nurse needed to do. I could see the sorrow on her face when she put the belongings in a bag. I wanted to ask for a dish, a cup, or a saucer—something to remind me of this beautiful little life that was gone—but I did not. She became part of my life, and I still hold her close to my heart.

There were so many tragic events I have witnessed. It seemed to go on and on. While life continued as usual on the outside, it was mind-blowing and traumatic on the inside. I can say without a doubt my bubble about life was torn completely apart. I was now fully aware of the horrific pain life could deal us and the vulnerabilities we had. It was terrifying. I made good friends with many wonderful parents while my son was in the hospital. Unfortunately, it had to be under such horrific circumstances. You bond with people who have children with bad hearts, cancer, abuse, accidents, and many more tragedies. The experience enables you to see such love and compassion that you sometimes are not fortunate enough to experience in everyday life. These tragedies open you up to how important life and family really are, and what they are truly all about. Unfortunately, some people never learn from their own circumstances. I witnessed many life-and-death experiences and will never forget the impacts they have on the families watching their loved ones suffer. It never leaves you.

There were so many nurses and doctors in the hospital in Brooklyn who had taken care of my precious little boy. I cannot say I found one doctor or nurse who did not give Daniel his or her all. These people were a gift from God. They helped in saving my son, along with the help of many prayers and my son's will to live the life he so much loved.

Daniel needed to have twenty-four-hour care at the beginning of his hospital stay. At that point, we needed to pay for a private nurse, and it was not covered under my husband's insurance plan. My family offered no financial help; I also did not receive any emotional or financial help from my husband's family, or even a hospital visit. My husband went to the bank and applied for a personal loan. When that ran out, he came in with an envelope with a large cash amount from his friends at work. We used it for Daniel's private care. When that ran out, these great, dedicated nurses each decided to take one shift for my son out of their own pockets. God bless them all!

> *For the love of money is the root of all kinds of evil. And some people, craving money, have wandered from the true faith and pierced themselves with many sorrows. (1 Timothy 6:10)*

Chapter 7

The Awakening

....

IT WAS THE beginning of August and I was in Daniel's room, like I had been every day for the last two months. The nurse came in and started to do the daily routine of taking his vitals, cleaning his bed, and checking his pupils to see how they were dilating. I was standing next to my son's bed, and the nurse was removing a bedpan that someone had left on his bedside table. The bedpan was not supposed to be there because he had a catheter inserted. The nurse picked it up to remove it and accidentally dropped it on the floor, causing it to make a very loud noise. They were not plastic like they are today; back then, they were made of aluminum and were quite heavy.

What happened next was a miracle. Daniel jumped in the bed, and his eyes opened wide. All I saw were his beautiful blue eyes staring up at the ceiling. I yelled to the nurse. She turned around and apologized for dropping the bedpan. I yelled to her, "Look! Daniel's eyes are open!" She came over, looked at him, and ran out of the room to call for the doctor.

The doctor rushed in and examined Daniel. He looked at his eyes and turned to me and said, "Daniel is coming out of his coma." My son was not moving at this point, but he had the biggest smile on his precious face. I kept telling him, "Mommy is here. I love you and need you so much." I kissed and hugged him over and over. Daniel was very aware I was by his side, he smiled whenever I talked to him. It was now approaching his third birthday, and he was out of his coma. At the time he awoke, I believed in my mind that he was going to be able to get up and walk and talk like before his accident. That did not happen. I considered myself to be a pretty level-headed woman back then, and although I was only twenty-one, I did not want to face anything other than to believe my son was going to be the same happy boy running around like he had before. I was in complete denial at that moment in time and was not dwelling on the recovery and the challenges he would be facing ahead.

After a full examination, the doctors informed me my son was out of his coma. His recovery was going to be slow, long, and very challenging. It was at that time I realized there was no more time for denial. My son's recovery needed my full attention. I welcomed all the doctors' advice. The surgeon told me at this time he never expected Daniel to survive. My baby boy was alive and ready to overcome all the challenges and obstacles put before him. I was so grateful to the life-saving doctors and nurses, the medical care my son had received, and the strength God gave me to continue moving forward.

> My child, never forget the things I taught you. Store my commands in your heart. If you do this, you will live many years, and your life will be very satisfying. Never let loyalty and kindness leave you! Tie them around your neck as a reminder. Write them deep within your heart. Then you will find favor with God and people, and you will earn a good reputation. (Proverbs 3:1-2-3-4)

The first couple of days, I spent my time holding my boy in my arms telling him how much I loved him. I talked about all the things he loved in his life. I could not believe how blessed I was to have him back, and I was going to be there for him every step of our new journey. I kept seeing the beautiful smile on his tiny, precious face, and it gave me so much hope. All the doctors involved in my son's care were excited at his impending recovery. I was informed by the doctor that they wanted to start weaning Daniel off the ventilator as soon as possible. I was told that if he did not reach this goal soon, he could be dependent on the tracheotomy for the rest of his life. The first day they tried to wean him from the ventilator was like watching someone putting a pillow over his face and smothering him. After a few short moments that seemed like a lifetime, the small plug that was inserted in his trachea was removed to allow Daniel to breathe. The tracheotomy was also what was used when inserting the tube to take out all the mucus from his little lungs. There are no words that could explain what it's like to see the person you love more than anything in the world suffering, and you can't do anything to help except watch him suffer. But it needed to be done so he would not be dependent on the ventilator.

The next day the nurse came in the room. She was there to repeat the same procedure that she had done on his tracheotomy the day before. She took the plug and inserted it in his trachea. Daniel struggled for a few seconds that seemed like a lifetime to me, and to our shock he started breathing on his own!

You have allowed me to suffer much hardships, but you will restore me to life again and lift me up to the depths of the earth. You will restore me to even greater honor and comfort me once again. (Psalms 71:20–21)

Citizens of heaven, where the lord Jesus Christ lives. And we are eagerly waiting for him to return as our savior. He will take our weak mortal bodies and change them into glorious bodies like his own, using the same power with which he will bring everything under his control. (Philippians 3:20–21)

A few weeks passed, and the doctor came in the room to inform me that Daniel was ready to be transferred to a rehab hospital within the next five days. I asked the doctor if I could take my son home before he was transferred; I had a strong need to be alone with him. The doctor suggested I not take him home, not only because it would be hard on me but also because he was concerned how Daniel had lived before his accident might affect him going home. The doctor believed he may still have some past memory and it might be difficult for Daniel to understand why he could not do the things he did before the accident. I insisted, and although he was hesitant, he complied with my wishes. I could not fathom what challenges we would have to face during those five days. I felt at that time that my love for my son would conquer all, but I was so wrong.

The hospital made arrangements for Daniel to return home by ambulance. When he came home, I was now fully aware that what the doctor had informed me of earlier was so true. The boy who left my home on June 7 was the same boy inside, but outside he was not walking, eating, or talking. He had so much pain trying to go to the bathroom, and he was not able to communicate by talking like he had before his accident. Daniel talked with his eyes and smiled whenever I asked him any questions. It was like his body was in an altered state, but his mind was aware of all his surroundings. He was aware I was his mother; his beautiful eyes and smile said it all. This was my hope to know he was the same precious son I gave birth to. He simply needed lots of love, patience and prayers to come back. I was dying inside to see my son lying there when just a few months before, he was a happy, healthy boy running around and free from any physical or mental challenges. I was now also back home with my husband, the man I wanted so badly to leave prior to the accident.

Five days passed, and Daniel and I made it through. Although it was heartbreaking, I was thankful to God for those five days alone with my son. It was now time to take him to the rehab hospital. I painfully packed his bags. This time we would be embarking on a much different journey.

We arrived at St. Mary's rehab early in the day and were greeted by the nuns who ran the hospital. They were gentle and very understanding, but I was also aware it was the doctors, nurses, and most important the therapists who were going to help Daniel learn to eat, talk, and use all the potential he had in him to function and move on. No bar was too high for him and he was truly the best patient ever. He was strong-willed, much like me. He loved life so much that I never doubted for a moment he would prevail.

Three things will last forever/ faith, hope, and love/ and the greatest of these is love. (1 Corinthians 13:13)

In the beginning it was hard on Daniel to adjust to me not staying overnight. I was his lifeline, but now I was only allowed to visit him a few times a week, and I brought him home every weekend. At this time my weight stayed down, at eighty-one pounds. As the months passed on, I continued my visits with my son at the hospital. One weekend I was informed by one of the nuns that I could not take him home for his regular weekend stay. The doctor looking over his care believed it was in my best interest to not allow him to go home. He felt my health was on the decline, and I needed the rest. If I became ill, then I would not be able to be there for my son. Although I understood his logic, I had my own. I needed my son as much as he needed me. That was how we both made it through from the very start of the trauma he sustained and into the start of his recovery. I had taken two buses and one train to the hospital, as I did every visit. This Friday, I took the return trip home without Daniel. When I returned home, I was physically and emotionally exhausted. I went to bed to escape the day's turmoil.

The phone rang, and I picked it up. It was my best friend Carol. She was aware by my voice that something was wrong. I explained to her the events that went on that day involving Daniel, and she reassured me over and over if I needed her for anything, she would be there, as she always was. My husband had come home by then. I was not paying any attention to him because he was coming home from one of the local taverns. He was using my son as an excuse for his addictions; the facts were he was doing this behavior well before my son's accident. All I could do was think about my boy and not being able to take him home. I was emotionally drained from guilt. I wanted to be with him, and I was having visions of him lying there in the hospital crib waiting for me.

I waited for my husband to fall asleep. It seemed like forever. I sat there and cried. It was around midnight when I picked up the phone to call my friend Carol. I asked her to take me to the rehab hospital, and she came right away to pick me up. She was my lifeline and was always there for me.

I walked in the front door of the rehab center around 1:00 a.m. and was greeted by a nun at the front desk. I explained to her what the outcome of my day was earlier when I went to see Daniel to take him home for our weekend visit together. Although she was very understanding, she stated that it was too late to visit at that hour. I insisted she contact the doctor so I could talk with him; I was not going to leave until I had access to my son. The nun reached the doctor and then handed me the phone. I told the doctor I appreciated his concern for my health and well-being, but I needed my son to be home with me. The doctor agreed without hesitation. I believed that he was expecting my phone call. He had taken a shot at trying to do the right thing. Although it had not worked out the way he wanted it to, I appreciated his concern.

> *Then Jesus turned to his disciples and said the kingdom of God is yours. God blesses you who are hungry now, for you will be satisfied. God blesses you who weep now, for in due time you will laugh. (Luke 6:20–21)*

I went down the long, dimly lit corridor until I approached the room Daniel was in, along with other children. I stood there at the entrance of the doorway and saw my little baby boy lying in his crib with a mesh cover over it. His tiny head was facing the window, looking out where the playground was, in the back of the building. The light from the moon against the dark sky was gleaming directly on him. It looked to me like a beautiful, soft halo was shimmering directly on his tiny face. I walked over to his crib and stood there in silence for a few moments. His beautiful blue eyes staring at the sky. Then he turned his head to my side as if he knew I was coming for him. He sensed my motherly presence. I was there. I come at just the right moment. Daniel was so elated with happiness that he turned his tiny head that had so much trauma months prior, now with no obstacles in his movement. Like a miracle, he was kicking his feet and waving his hand just like when he was a baby. I picked up my boy, and I hugged and kissed him over and over. It was like we were both thrown a life preserver. The love we shared and the bond we had was like no other in my lifetime. Daniel was my miracle boy.

When Jesus saw his mother standing beside the disciple he loved he said to her, "Dear woman here is your son" and he said to this disciple, "Here is your mother" and from then on the disciple took her into his home. (John 19:26–27)

The nurse came in the room to help me dress my son, and off we went home. This weekend was going to be a turning point in our lives because we had overcame the obstacle that there would be no more confusion about taking Daniel back to our home for his weekend visits. We were a team, and our bond would never be broken. Every day was a gift. From this day on, I did not spend much time thinking of anything else but helping my son with his recovery. Everything else became unimportant. I believed every obstacle we had to face together would be won by Daniel's positive outlook and strong will to survive.

Daniel's main rehab therapist was compassionate and kind. She was a small-built Asian woman and spent nearly every day with him teaching him the basics skills that he needed in life to be as independent as possible: picking up a spoon, learning to speak words again, and standing up in a square box for hours to strengthen his weak legs. These are many things people take for granted, Daniel had therapy every day. It was painful and exhausting, but as always, he never complained. When he came home for his weekend visits, we worked very hard together to continue his goal to recovery. This continued up to his release from rehab ten months later.

> *He gives power to the weak and strength to the powerless. Even youths will become weak and tired and young men will fall in exhaustion. But those who trust in the LORD will find new strength. They will soar high on wings like eagles. They will run and not grow weary. They will walk and not be faint. (Isaiah 40:29-31)*

I never did reunite with Daniel's biological father. We would not have contact for many years, I needed to give all my time, attention, and focus to my son. Daniel and I needed our strength for the long, hard road we had to face together; this was our journey. God gave my son a second chance at life, and he gave me a second chance at motherhood. I was going to do everything I could to honor this special gift God allowed us to experience. We were given this journey full of life and love to travel together. I came to find out this Journey we were on was not all that I thought it would be. Unfortunately, my son and I were not excluded from experiencing other adversity.

Chapter 8

End of Rehab

DANIEL WAS COMING to the end of his rehab. It was May 1969, approaching nearly ten months since he was admitted. The doctor started talking to me about discharging him around June. He believed everyone involved with my son's care had come as far as they could with his rehab. The rest was up to him, with my help. Although I was very scared, I was also overwhelmed with happiness. I was so alone at home without my son, and the thought of him returning home gave me so much hope for the future. All the time Daniel was in rehab, my husband and I were not connected in any way—no love, no intimacy, no communication. We were worlds apart. Most of my time at home was spent trying to keep busy and to not harbor all the guilt and shame that had entered my life since my son's accident.

The month before my son was going to be released from rehab, the doctor stated that I should consider having another child. I informed the doctor that I was not only unhappy in my marriage at that moment, but I had been unhappy from the start of it. I basically told him my marriage was doomed. He continued to express to me that another child could bring happiness not only for me but also for Daniel. He told me that the child could help my son to grow at a higher rate mentally and physically. I had no plans at any time to have a child. It was not until time passed that I was able to completely comprehend what the doctor's words meant—and how right he was.

> *The Lord says I will guide you along the pathway for your*
> *life. I will advise you and watch over you (Psalm 32:8)*

I had grown so much in the year my little boy was hospitalized. I realized every moment was important in life, and it also could be cut short in a blink of an eye. I now had one month before Daniel's release from rehab to prepare for his arrival. After I left the rehab, I was so excited about the reality of my son finally returning home. I was elated with joy and happiness. The rehab hospital was a godsend in my son's recovery.

My husband and I were still living under the same roof and trying to be civil to each other. I tried not to allow anything he did affect me; I was only concerned with my son. The reality of him coming home gave me an awakening. The less bitter I tried to be, the more at peace I was, and I needed that to help me to get through. I felt I needed to try anything to salvage some of this broken relationship, if I could.

Here I was, severely underweight, and I had no physical contact with my husband in a very long time. In the midst of all these changes and mixed emotions, I became intimate with my husband only twice in the month of May. This had no bearing on my having a child with my husband like the doctor had suggested. I was only concerned about my son's recovery, and I wanted to make some peace for the sake of my long journey ahead. Then just as fast as it happened, it stopped. I tried to feel compassion for him, but with all that conspired in our marriage, I still could not have feelings of love. So many bad things were said and done, and he was still giving in to his addictions.

With all that was happening, I enrolled in a beauty school part time to help keep me busy on the days I did not go to the rehab hospital. The time when I was home was so lonely and miserable. I missed Daniel being with me and sharing our life together. In between my school classes, I planned on Daniel's homecoming. It was finally going to be a reality. I was going to evening classes two days a week. During one of my classes, I started to feel very weak, dizzy, and sick to my stomach. I related not feeling well to the fact I was underweight, undernourished, tired, and working around many different hair products.

I went home early that night from class. In the next few days, I continued to feel dizzy. I then decided to make an appointment with the doctor. After an exam and some tests, the doctor chalked my feeling sick to be from anticipation and anxiety regarding Daniel's coming home. I then continued to prepare for my son's homecoming. That was my key objective: to concentrate on the true love of my life, my baby boy. A few days later, the phone rang, and it was the doctor. He informed me that the symptoms I had were due to my test coming back positive. He told me I was pregnant. I was floored. He told me all the stress from my marriage and Daniel's accident caused my body to come to many different crossroads due to all the trauma I was experiencing. When I was told I was having my son released from rehab, the doctor stated I was finally so at peace that my body was able to accept the conception during the few times of my intimacy. I never imagined having another child when my husband and I were intimate. I never gave it a thought, especially with my life, my marriage, and my health being in such turmoil.

> *Elizabeth gave a glad cry and explained to Mary, "God has blessed you among all woman, and your child is blessed. Why am I so honored that the mother of my Lord should visit me? When I heard your greeting, the baby in my womb jumped for joy. You are blessed because you believed the Lord would do as he said." (Luke 1:42)*

My pregnancy was bittersweet. I was so elated, but at the same time I was so afraid that I may not be able to take care of my son, who was now physically and mentally challenged. Daniel was coming home in a few short weeks and needed special care. I did not want my pregnancy to hinder his recovery. I never had one doubt in my mind that my son wouldn't progress and prevail. It was my guilt that kept creeping back. Time would be taken away from him—time he needed and deserved to move forward. As quickly as these feelings came, they went. First I was overwhelmed and then overjoyed. I came to realize the part of me being riddled with guilt would never completely leave. Guilt became part of who I was; I simply needed to learn to live with it. I was already doing this for quite some time.

> *Wash me clean from my guilt. Purify me from my sin. For I recognize my rebellion; it haunts me day and night. Against you, and you alone, have I sinned; I have done what is evil in your sight. You will be proved right in what you say, and your judgment against me is just. For I was born a sinner— yes, from the moment my mother conceived me. But you desire honesty from the womb, teaching me wisdom even there. Purify me from my sins, and I will be clean; wash me, and I will be whiter than snow. Oh, give me back my joy again; you have broken me— now let me rejoice. Don't keep looking at my sins. Remove the stain of my guilt. Create in me a clean heart, O God. Renew a loyal spirit within me. Do not banish me from your presence, and don't take your Holy Spirit from me. Restore to me the joy of your salvation, and make me willing to obey you. (Psalm 51:2-12)*

Daniel was permanently wheelchair-bound, paralyzed on his right side with limited mobility to his right leg. He also lost all mobility to his right arm and hand. Daniel could not walk, he was gaining strength to sit up, and he had trouble with his speech. He was totally dependent on everyone to dress, eat, or toilet himself. These were things he was able to do before the accident. It was now June 1969, one year after Daniel's accident. He arrived home, and my pregnancy went forward. My marriage was at a standstill, and my husband's addiction was still as strong as ever. It dominated everything in his life.

Chapter 9

Daniel's Strong Will to Recover

DANIEL AND I stayed home for the first six months of my pregnancy. The only time I went out was when I went shopping or had my doctor's appointments. My best friend Carol came over and watched Daniel for me. The time I was home with my son was spent retraining him to use the potty. Day after day, hour after hour, reading book after book, my patient son mastered the art of the potty. He was so happy and proud of himself. What a glorious day! He was my hero. We laughed, cried, and clapped hands. We were a winning team. Daniel and I both worked on his speech day after day. By now he was saying the word I longed to hear again: he called me Ma. What was once taken for granted in life only two months before his third birthday was now a goal he had fought for and won.

My husband would come home mostly on weekends smelling like alcohol and perfume. This may sound like an old cliché' but he did have lipstick on his collar. It may be hard to believe, but I truly did not care my husband was never home. I was simply happy with my son being alive and me not having had to bury him in 1968. Life to me was beautiful now. God's second gift to me, was my pregnancy.

I was now over my morning sickness. I started to eat better little by little, and I took my vitamins. I did not smoke or drink alcohol; I was not into all that back then. However, the first three months of the pregnancy, I did lose two pounds. Then after my first trimester, my weight and appetite improved. Thank God, because I looked so pitifully frail. I was feeling somewhat embarrassed that people were becoming aware about my pregnancy and the fact that I had been intimate with my husband in the frail condition I was in. I realized that kind of thinking was so unimportant with what I was dealing with in my life, but at that time I had to learn to channel my negative feelings in a more positive way. The doctor believed my pregnancy saved my life. Before I became pregnant, I would eat and feel some comfort for a short time, and then the pain and guilt came creeping back, so I would throw it all up. Now I had to care for not only my son but my unborn baby, who needed nutrition. The bottom line was I was both of their lifelines. I had to continue on my journey for the plan and purpose God had for me and my children.

Although I stayed home for the six months and the doctor did not want me lifting my now four-year-old son, I needed to get him out. My family was nowhere in sight to help, and neither were most of my so-called friends, who disappeared when the accident happened, with the exception of Carol. I was always so proud to have Carol in my life and to witness what a special woman she was. She had a beautiful voice to go along with all her God-given talents. There was no doubt that if I ever needed her, she would always be there for Daniel and me. We had been inseparable since early childhood. She was a true gem.

I then decided to go against doctor's orders, and I started taking Daniel out for some much-needed fresh air. He needed to see people and enjoy the life he loved and had missed. I put my faith in God to protect me and my unborn child. So I put my son in the carriage I had specially made from a store in my Brooklyn neighborhood, and I started to go out day after day. We went walking, shopping, eating out, visiting my small circle of friends, and loving life again. I depended every day on God to help me through, and he did.

The Lord replied my precious, precious child. I love you and I would never leave you during your times of trial and suffering. When you see only one set of footprints, it was then that I carried you. I read this poem often and it is what God has done for me since 1968. —Margaret Fishback Powers

A month before my baby's arrival, my ailing mom came to stay with me for a few weeks. It was my turn to be with her, although I never minded having her with me. It came down to only two sisters out of six helping with Mom; the other four were always busy with their husbands and children. My mother never had much support from those daughters and two of her sons, but there was always my brother Frankie, who was a loving, kind soul. He adored our mother and always watched out for her. Mom protected my brother like I protected Daniel.

One night while Mom was visiting, my husband went out to the local tavern after work. I did not want him coming home intoxicated, so I decided to go after him at eight months pregnant and ask him to come home. Later on that evening, after I found him, we exchanged a few choice words at the tavern, and I went home alone. It was several hours later when he came strolling in. I was still up, and so was Mom. Daniel was sound asleep. I ran to the side entrance door that he always entered through when he came home. When I greeted him at the hallway entrance, he never said a word to me; he put his two hands on my face and twisted my cheeks until I thought they would fall off, and he told me to never come looking for him again. I would not make a sound because I did not want to wake Daniel or upset my mother. At that very moment, I despised him more than ever, and I wanted to end this farce of a marriage. I did not want him to exist along with all the heavy baggage that he had. After this incident, I made a promise to myself that one day I was going to find some way out and move on. I could have had my labor brought on by his actions, and it would have put my unborn baby in danger. My mom apologized so many times for encouraging me to marry him, and I always told her it was not her decision; it was mine.

Chapter 10

Baby's Arrival

I WAS NOW in my ninth month of pregnancy, and the doctor was convinced I was having a boy; he felt that way early on. In those days they had no sonograms. The doctor based this on my size and the position of the baby. Most of my small circle of friends were rooting for a girl, and they believed the girl's arrival would be more helpful to me than a boy. All this meant nothing to me. I was so happy that I made it to full term, and as long as the baby was healthy, I did not care whether I had a boy or a girl. I also gained back all my lost weight, plus some.

The time for delivery was here, and I started having contractions. They lasted three days until finally they were two and a half to three minutes apart. I called my doctor, and he informed me to stay at home. I was worried and took it upon myself to call the hospital to express my concerns and fears. I explained what my doctor had told me. The hospital's reply to me was to get there immediately. I arrived at the hospital at around 5:20 a.m. There was no time for the usual preparation before the birth. The doctor was notified by the hospital and was on his way. He arrived and started putting marks on my stomach. I asked him what he was doing, and he told me he was going to give me a C-section. My water had not even broken, and I demanded he break it. I was not going to have a C-section. The doctor complied and moments later my baby was delivered. All I asked the nurse was whether my baby was healthy, and was it a boy? Her reply was, the baby is healthy and "It's a girl, six pounds five ounces. Born 6:05 a.m." Thank God! I had watched a soap opera for years. One of my favorite characters was a beautiful, strong woman named Laura. Although the soap was a fantasy, it was a diversion from my everyday activities, so I named my daughter after her.

My mom and sister watched Daniel for the three days I was in the hospital. My husband never took off from work, but Mom made sure Daniel was safe and well taken care of. It would be the second time I had left him since his rehab stay. I missed him so much while I was in the hospital, and I worried every moment that he would get injured again. I delivered at the same hospital I had my son five years earlier. If it was not for the great care and expertise from the nurses that I called when I was in labor, I would have given birth to my daughter at home. My sister came to pick me up at the hospital along with my husband. We then went to my other sister's house, where my mother was staying with Daniel. It was to be a very small gathering with the family. The day I brought my daughter home, Daniel was overjoyed with love and excitement for his new baby sister.

> *You were cleansed from your sins when you obeyed the truth,*
> *so now you must show sincere love to each other as brothers*
> *and sisters. Love each other deeply with all your heart.*
> *(1Peter 1:22)*

When I reflect back to when I gave birth to my daughter, I remember looking through the nursery window in disbelief and thinking to myself how blessed I was to have my son alive, and now I had a healthy, baby girl. When I went back to the doctor for my six-week checkup, I was not too happy at being there. The doctor stated to me he was surprised that I had a girl. My reply to him was

I was simply grateful to have a healthy baby. When I left his office, I knew I was never going back due to his complete lack of concern when he suggested I stay home after having labor pains for three days, and also when they were two minutes apart on the early morning of my delivery. These were major red flags for me.

Chapter 11

Back Home

....

THINGS STARTED TO become increasingly strained with my marriage when I came home with my daughter. I was in so much pain and discomfort from the delivery while attending to my newborn daughter and my son that I pleaded with my husband to give me some help with the baby. His answer to me was, "She is probably not mine either."

It was only a matter of time. I was praying that this part of my life could be put behind me. Although I had been hoping for this for some time, I still counted my blessings that life was good to me, bad marriage and all. Although I resented his addiction, I never blamed myself for his problem. I had enough blame to go around for my own wrong decisions. I continued to take care of my two children on my own the majority of time. That was okay. I was better off that way, and so were the children. I continued to stay in survival mode.

The apartment I lived in had two wonderful landlords. They were kind and very compassionate about what I was going through. When I moved in, my son was eight months old, and I was still living there when he had his accident. They also witnessed my pregnancy and my daughter's arrival home. Shortly after my daughter's birth, my landlord decided to buy a home directly across the street. I was approached by them and asked if I was interested in purchasing their home for myself and my children. I had some money I had put together on my own over the years and put in a joint account. (Big Mistake)

After I talked with my landlord's wife, I was very excited at the possibility of purchasing the home. I went into the dresser drawer, and the bank book was in the same place, deep in the back and under my clothes. I opened it up, and there were no funds available. The withdrawals were made over time when Daniel was hospitalized. I believe in my husband's mind, he felt by dipping into the bank account here and there, I would not notice the funds missing due to my mental state at that horrific time. Although my landlords were very kind and understanding, they still needed to sell their home to purchase their new one. Of course my husband was trying to blame my son's accident on his demons, but I knew better, and so did everyone else. Now I had to prepare to move out before the sale. I had no doubt God's purpose was for me to be where I was at that place in time with my son and daughter.

I was now making a move with my five-year-old son and my five-month-old daughter to my sister's small apartment. My sister was a single mom with two small boys of her own. My hope was to be there for a short time. My husband also came to the apartment. My sister did not like him in any way, shape, or form from the start of my marriage, and she did not have many kind things to say about him.

Chapter 12

The Start of the System

WHILE STILL LIVING with my sister, I had a doctor's appointment for Daniel to keep up with his recovery, and to monitor the seizures he was now experiencing as a result of his head trauma. Back in those days, head trauma was diagnosed as cerebral palsy. The doctor informed me about a program that might benefit my son. Daniel was five years old now, and he needed interaction with other children his age to continue to learn self-help skills. The year was 1970, and I had an appointment that was set up for me to meet a social worker in Brooklyn. I was not happy with going to this location because it was not considered a good neighborhood.

I needed to bring my daughter that day, and while she was being attended to by staff in a small playroom, my son and I were interviewed for a chance to have him attend the program. I was being asked many questions about Daniel. The social worker was very concerned about my appearance and weight, as was the principal who also interviewed my son and me. The stress of taking care of my son and daughter caused me to lose the weight I had gained during my pregnancy. The program was being run by two compassionate people. They told me that if Daniel was accepted to attend, this location would only be for a brief time. There were plans for a brand-new building opening in another part of Brooklyn. It would be very spacious with a built-in swimming pool, rehab center, special needs classes, and much more. It was not far from a police station, which made me feel somewhat secure. After the interview was over, I was informed by the social worker and the program director that I would be notified in approximately thirty days regarding Daniel's acceptance into the program. I went home with my hopes high, but not high enough to be let down.

I was only in the door of my sister's apartment for a short time when the phone rang. It was the social worker informing me that the principle of the program made a decision after Daniel and I had left. She believed he was a good candidate for their school day treatment program and would also allow me to spend time with my daughter and to address my poor health condition. She was also concerned that there were things in my life that needed to be addressed. Although I was very scared about the new adventure my son was going on. I was also very concerned about his long traveling time on the bus. It would take approximately one and a half hours to arrive at the program, possibly longer, because there were other children being picked up at different locations.

My fears were very real, and I was given reassurance that a matron would be on the bus every day. Her role was to oversee and tend to the children while the bus driver was driving. It would only be for a few months until the new building was completed. I was so terrified to leave him with someone else again. I never felt at ease leaving him since the accident. Even when I went to the store, I couldn't wait to get home and make sure he was okay. Knowing the matron was going to be with him on the bus gave me a little comfort, but my fears were so deep I knew it would take some time to regain some kind of comfort level. I knew I couldn't shelter him forever and hold him back from going out in the world again. This new adventure he was going on would be the third time we would again be separated since his rehab stay. I had faith he would tolerate the bus trip and be safe.

This is my command—be strong and courageous. Do not be afraid or discouraged for the lord your God is with you wherever you go. (Joshua 1:9)

The first day of program came. The bus arrived at approximately 6:30 a.m. The bus driver and matron greeted Daniel and introduced themselves. Then they put him on the bus lift. I watched him being taken up while holding his brand-new lunchbox on his lap. Then he was placed on the very back of the bus so he could look out the window. Daniel was secured with his seat belt and his wheelchair strapped down to the floor so it could not move. My heart was breaking. I did not want to let him go, but I knew I needed to. I was so scared and felt like I was deserting him, although I knew I was not. I still felt my enemy, guilt, hovering over me. Then I spent a few more brief minutes with the bus driver and matron, talking and getting acquainted with them, and I gave them some information on Daniel. At that moment it brought back the memory of when my son was in rehab, and I went to the hospital late at night to bring him home and found him looking out the window toward the sky and the moon. I could see him sitting sideways on the bus waving to me, and the love I felt at that moment in time was indescribable. He was my little boy, I was supposed to protect him—and I did not at the time of his accident. But here he was, still so trusting, loving, and caring. With all this, he still loved me unconditionally.

I waved good-bye to my son, and I watched as the bus went down the street on that early, dark morning in December to take him on his new journey to his new program. My heart was truly broken. I thought of all my boy had to endure because of my one horrific decision to leave him in the park with my sister. My thoughts were of how much I loved him and how sorry I was. I cried all day. Although I now had my daughter, it did not ease my pain or guilt.

Have mercy on me Lord, I am in distress. Tears blur my
eyes, my body and soul are withering away. I am dying form
grief, my years are shortened by sadness, sin has drained my
strength, I am wasting away from within. (Psalm 31:7–10)

The weeks went by, and then several months. Daniel was doing very well in his new program. Not long after that, I was given the opportunity to be able to look at the designs for the new building to see the real deal. There was going to be so much more available for the physically and mentally challenged. This was going to be a state-of-the-art project. Now that I was able to see this newly built school was going to be a reality, I felt more secure knowing my son was going to be attending his program for only a short-time.

Chapter 13

The Move

FINALLY AFTER SEVERAL months of residing with my sister, I was able to move to my own apartment again. While I was residing at my sister's. I was able to save money from my husband's stamp money he had received from his job. I called it gift money or bonus money; it made my getting by much easier than depending on his salary, which I did not receive most of the time. Although my new place was not in the neighborhood I was raised in, I was relieved to have my own privacy back. It was only a few miles from my old neighborhood, and I fit in very well with the new neighbors. My only mistake was I had taken an apartment on a second-floor walk-up in a private house. This meant I had to carry Daniel up and down the stairs every day to put him on the bus and take him off. I was young and strong, so I did it. I was still with my husband and was hoping the move may change things for the family again. How wrong I was. He had taken a second job in my old neighborhood as a weekend bartender a short time after we moved in. It was only part time, and when he worked days Monday to Friday, he never came home on time after work and sometimes did not come home for days.

The true love of my life, Daniel's biological father, was gone for a long time. My love for him was the force that kept my hope up to continue, so that one day we may reunite again. I met quite a few good people in my new neighborhood, but I also went back to my old neighborhood often. I would send Daniel off to school and take my daughter with me to meet up with my old friends.

Daniel was now finally attending his new school day program. It was so beautiful and was equipped with all the needs for the disabled. So many wonderful things happened over those years. We had great memories from meeting such fantastic people: teachers, directors, social workers, teachers' aides, therapists, volunteers, bus drivers, matrons, and security guards, along with a top-notch principal and social worker. These wonderful people were such a support system to my family and me, but most of all they always looked out for my son's welfare. Daniel created lifelong friendships, especially with his best friend, a young African American boy with a beautiful spirit and a heart of gold. They went on trips, did activities, talent shows, attended swimming events, and had both graduated together from their high school program to an adult program. They were years of pure love, fun, and commitment from all involved. Daniel learned to do arts and crafts and work in the wood shop, he made some beautiful things for me, especially around Mother's Day and my birthday. He learned to write, count money, and so much more.

Chapter 14

The Other Woman

WHILE I WAS residing in the new neighborhood, my husband met the other woman. He would go to work and then on the way home stop off at different local taverns. After two years I decided to move back to my old neighborhood and put my roots back down. My marriage was still no better and never would be. I decided now that my son was older and my daughter was two and a half, it was time for me to move on and end the marriage at last. I did not allow it to affect me personally because I was not in love with him; to be honest, I didn't even like him. I felt I was going to unload a ton of baggage. There were many people who did not understand my feelings on this matter; they believed I should have showed anger. I believed that out of this unhealthy marriage union, a beautiful baby girl was produced by God's grace. She was Daniel's gift, and he loved his sister so much. Their bond was a miracle for me to witness every day.

I settled in my new apartment in Brooklyn. It was a three-room walk-in in a newly built home with a small yard. It was there that I truly felt I was home again. My rent back then was only two hundred dollars a month, with gas and electric included. I had two great landlords, and they treated me with great respect. I decided to move into my apartment without my husband. I was willing to do it in order to have my children live in a home that was not continually disrupted. It was worth any sacrifice.

I had taken a job at a hospital as a switchboard operator close to my home. I was very fortunate to have a very sweet next-door neighbor to help take care the children from 2:30–5:00 p.m. Although I was not living with my husband, I worked it out with him to relieve the sitter after his work day was over only for a few weeks, until my training was over.

Then the phone calls started coming from the babysitter that he was not showing up to relieve her. She explained she could not stay the night. My shift was 3:00–11:00 p.m. This was now becoming very stressful given the fact that Daniel needed special care and my daughter was only two and a half. I was not receiving any financial help from my husband and was going to be in deep trouble without a job. When I told him this, he told me to go on public assistance. He informed me his girlfriend was on public assistance herself along with her two boys, and they were doing very well. My bosses did not want me to leave, I was doing so well in my training and they were willing to make any allowances for me to stay. The people who worked with me were aware of how hard I was trying to keep my position.

Those who won't care for their relatives, especially those in their own household have denied the true faith. Such people are worse than unbelievers. (1 Timothy 5:8)

I finally quit my job and decided that I really had no other option but to go for financial help, against my better wishes. I truly tried to make it work, but I was also neglecting my children. My landlord was very understanding to my situation, because he and his wife resided upstairs. He also cooperated with the public assisted agency so I could receive help for my rent, food, and clothing. I was very humbled by their kindness and understanding. They became like surrogate parents to me. It became a real home to me and for my children. Although our place was small, we loved it and made it work. All in all, I wound up spending seven years in that apartment I called home.

I continued to raise my son and daughter the best way I could, although the challenges were still coming with Daniel involving his care, concerns about his seizure disorder, medications, back problems, and overall health. He continued to progress to the best of his ability. I look back now and can say they were the best times of my life. Unfortunately, many times I felt defeated, tired, and drained. I would do anything now to have it all back. I did not know it then, but those were the good old days.

> *Give your burdens to the Lord, and he will take care of you.*
> *He will not permit the Godly to slip and fall (Psalm 55:22)*

Through a friend I was introduced to a man. He was divorced nine years and was an active New York City police officer, having spent ten years on the job. As the weeks and months passed, little by little I allowed myself to open up with him. One day out of the blue, a call came in at my home. It was from my husband's girlfriend. First I was taken aback by her call, and I asked what she wanted. She asked me why I was still married. Before I could reply, she stated to me that my husband informed her he couldn't get divorced from me because I had cancer. I laughed and told her, "Good luck. You'll need it with him." I hung up. A short while later, I received another phone call, and this time I did not hang up. I listened to her, and she was very distraught and stated my husband was gambling and carousing with other women. She told me she could not take it any longer. I informed her his bad behavior was his way of being uncommitted to their relationship, due to his unhealthy addictions. I then told her that I never had cancer, and it was another one of his lies. I felt sad for her and believed she really loved this conflicted man.

Eventually my new boyfriend paid for me to file and receive my divorce. Now I could have closure and move on. I was finally able to rid myself of my husband and have some happiness. My boyfriend and I married just two weeks after my divorce became final. Many people considered this to be too soon, but my marriage was done a long time before that. Although my new companion was far from a perfect role model he was a very responsible man who loved my son and daughter, and he treated them like his very own. I often wondered many times over the years what I would have been like if I would never have met my ex-husband, and if it would have worked out with Daniel's father. The answer I always came up with was that I would not have given birth to my sweet baby girl. It was all in God's plan.

By now my ex was fading away and hardly seeing the children. It was very sad to hear Daniel asking for Daddy, which he called my ex all the time. My daughter would ask the same. Innocent children subjected to abandonment. He was now off supporting his girlfriend and her two boys. That was a hard pill for me to swallow, especially from this man, who once stated to me my son was not his and maybe not even my daughter. For unknown reasons, he never believed he should be a committed parent or financially responsible to the children.

Years later he made a connection with my daughter in her late teens, but he still believed the same parental obligations stood meaning. The title of deadbeat dad was never going away. The true facts are he never had any problems with financing the gambling casinos, the horses, or the slot machines, and he showed more attention to his girlfriend and her children than to his own. I do know he gave them much more than he ever gave my family. As time passed, she did marry my ex, and she remains married to him to this day. Unknown to me back then, this woman would become a major lifeline, to my family, and most of all Daniel. When the social services would catch up with him at his workplace in an attempt to get child support, his workplace moved him to another site—another system failure. Then social services had to start the process all over again. He never voluntarily paid. It wasn't until years later that he would have his income tax checks garnished for back pay that went to the state when I was receiving help from a public assistance agency. The Iron workers union was certainly not looking out for families back then; when I went to them personally, it fell upon deaf ears. I will say hats off to the social services in my hometown of New York City. They were more kind and giving than my own family including my daughter's father's family. .

Over the years of my marriage, there were many obstacles we had to face, and we overcame them. My husband and I went looking for a house. We did not have much money back then, but we wanted to have a place we could call our own for my son and daughter. Daniel was now fourteen, and Laura was nine. It was now becoming crowded in my three-room apartment

We finally found a tiny house approximately twenty blocks from my apartment. Although the house was small, it was like a castle to me. After a few minor obstacles that came our way in the purchase of our home, we were able to move in several months later. Laura was still able to attend her Catholic grammar school, and Daniel was doing great in his day program; at home he kept moving forward. Life was good and the children were happy. I felt I reached one of my many goals, although there were many others to face.

Chapter 15

Daniel's Surgery

TIME PASSED, AND Daniel was turning sixteen when we went to see a neurosurgeon. I was informed it was time for him to have a plate inserted in the left side of his skull to cover the portion that was shattered and removed after the accident; there was only skin covering and protecting his brain. To protect Daniel, he needed to wear a helmet every day, and the surgery would eliminate that. At the time of his accident, I was informed that one day this was going to be needed for my son's safety, but one still didn't think of it until it became a reality.

The arrangements were made for Daniel to have surgery. We were quite familiar with the hospital because he was an outpatient in the seizure clinic; and also had several past surgeries. The side effect of his seizure medications was the overgrowth of his gums covering his teeth. He had to have surgery to cut his gums back. It was so painful for him, but as always he never complained. This took me back to 1968 again. All my fears and guilt came flooding back like a tidal wave of emotions. I was terrified he was going to die. I had to put my faith in this good hospital and God that it was going to be okay.

Faith is the confidence that what we hope for will actually happen,' It gives us assurance about things we cannot see. (Hebrews 11:1)

The day came for the surgery, and Daniel was a trooper as always. After he was prepped and his head was shaved, I hugged and kissed him and reassured him everything was going to be okay. The surgeon told me the surgery should take approximately three hours. I waited in the small waiting room with some family who stayed with me. I paced back and forth for what seemed like forever. Finally the surgeon came into the waiting room to talk with me and told me the operation was not a success. I was in shock. The anesthesiologist explained to me he had administered enough anesthesia to put down a horse, but Daniel would not go out. They felt it was too much of a risk to give him more. I was then told it would be in his best interest to wait two years, and then they would try again.

Daniel was so strong mentally and physically. He would fight anything to survive. Putting him under the knife was not what he wanted. I believe it could have something to do with him being in a coma after his accident. The surgeon stated he was stressed out and trying again to soon would cause him too much anxiety. I was relieved he was okay, I hoped the operation would have been a success. Although Daniel did not like to wear his helmet, having brain surgery to eliminate that was very scary for him. The reason why it had taken so many years before the plate was to be inserted was due to the fact that the brain and skull needed to grow to his adult size. We went home and continued life as before, hoping the next time it would be easier on everyone most of all Daniel.

My daughter was now eleven years old and was extremely close to her brother. She cooked for him, dressed him, and even gave him his seizure medications. They did everything together. She always had her friends over and included Daniel in everything she did. Her friends were so good to him; he was one of the gang. Laura was always very popular, and there were so many people in her and Daniel's lives. They watched movies together, listened to music, played board games, and rode their big wheels around the block. We lived in a tightly knit neighborhood. Everyone knew and looked out for each other like family. Laura was so mature and knowledgeable. It was amazing how she made friends so easily and bonded with them. At age nine she would go to the neighborhood food chain store down the block from our house, taking along her shopping cart and picking out all the sale items. At age eleven she put a large four-foot pool filter together. She was a little jack of all trades. She could do so much, but her true gift in life was giving and caring. My husband sent my daughter to private school, paying her tuition with no help from her biological father. My husband was looking out for my daughter's happiness as any good father would want for their child.

Watching my son and daughter growing up was a miracle in itself. They bonded so well together. As she explored her world and starting learning about it, he watched her every move. When she starting to crawl, her brother would sit up and move himself with his one arm (Daniel's right arm was paralyzed from the accident) to imitate her. As she started to feed herself, he copied her, and when she started talking, he did as well. Although slightly altered, Daniel was able to completely regain his speech and then some. He said whatever he wanted no matter where he was. To see them bond together was so special. My daughter became her brother's teacher. They crawled, ate, and talked together. When she cried, he cried; when she laughed, he laughed. They shared their friends, went on trips, and went to each other's school functions. They were a team and were best friends. This is what the doctor from the rehab hospital had meant all those years ago, when he stated to me after my son's accident that having another child would help him develop to his full potential. My connection to my ex-husband gave me my daughter, and my connection to my new husband gave my family love and stability. God gave me the tools I needed at the time to survive, and then my daughter came along and gave so much light and joy to Daniel and my darkness.

> We know what real love is because Jesus gave up his life for us. So we ought to give up our lives for our brother and sisters. If someone has enough money to live well and sees a brother or sister in need but shows no compassion—how can God's love be in that person? (1 John 3:16–17)

Two years had passed since the first attempt to insert the plate in Daniels skull. Now it was time to bring him back to try again, and hopefully this time would be a success. The doctor was going to sedate my son mildly before he was prepared for surgery. That was not done on the first try, and the doctor believed that is what contributed to his anxiety. Before the surgery, I spent time with my son and tried to reassure him as best as I could that everything would be okay. We did not want a repeat of the first attempt. It needed to be done for his safety, and to eliminate his need to wear the helmet. Daniel went for the second time. He never complained or showed anxiety on the outside, but inside I was aware he was anxious. I prayed to God this time around it would work.

After what seemed like forever, the doctor came in the waiting room three hours later and informed me the plate was inserted successfully. He also informed me that it was mesh, not metal. I was elated. I ran upstairs just in time to watch Daniel come out of the operating room on the way to recovery. Not surprisingly, he was sitting up and waving to me. The surgeon was floored. The doctor stated the amount of anesthesia and relaxing medications were enough to keep him out for some time. Not my son—I knew him better. He was a tough nut to crack and was strong-willed. He was so happy to get rid of his helmet. Although he had to wear it for a short time after the surgery for the healing process, he was okay with that. The doctor now wanted to address another medical problem my son was having: as a result of the car accident, he had a curved spine. Several inserts were made for his wheelchair to help him to sit up straight, but none of them worked. The doctor felt it would be good to insert a steel rod in his spine. I spent endless days and nights thinking of this major decision, and I declined. I was informed it would be much worse as he became older, but I stuck to my decision. I was not only fearful of the surgery but was informed it was not without big risk. Thankfully over the years, the spine curvature stayed the same and did not hinder his health. The doctor's biggest worry was that if the spine curved too much, it could lean against Daniel's lungs and heart. The doctor watched it very carefully as Daniel aged.

Chapter 16

Daniel Entering the System

DANIEL CONTINUED TO flourish in his day treatment program, as well as at home. With the exception of a few short stays, he was admitted into two different rehabs in his teen years. One was in New York City, and the second was in upstate New York. These were opportunities to give him extensive therapy and to allow him to see if he could ever be able to walk again, even with assistance. After the two stays, the doctor informed me that was never going to be an option. My son was resigned to the fact that he would not walk again, but he also made me feel it was okay. I was so grateful to God for allowing my son to be with me every day. Daniel was continuing to do very well, and my daughter was growing into a fine young lady who never stopped protecting her brother. If anyone would make remarks to him or about him concerning his disability, she would fire back. Laura was witty and very mature for her age.

Daniel's best friend was living with Catholic Charities for many years in a group home. Eventually he was moved into a group home residence run by the same agency where he attended his day treatment program with my son. While he was with Catholic Charities, my husband, Daniel, and I would visit him many times. My son and his best friend had such a strong bond that I believed nothing could separate them. They were closer than brothers could ever hope to be. I was not fortunate enough to have met with his family, but he always said such kind things about them. When the time came to go home, I was always thankful to go. The group home setting made me feel very sad because it lacked that homey feeling I had in my own house. It did not matter if my son and I traveled to his best friend's group home, or other friends' homes. Our home was always our safe haven.

"There are "friends", who destroy each other, but a real friend sticks closer than a brother." (Proverbs 18:24)

I believe Catholic Charities had the best intentions in running their group home setting with the budget that the nuns were given. Going on these visits every other week was the highlight of Daniel's day. Our visits were always productive for them, and that was what mattered. The group home housed many residents who were living in small rooms. I would definitely have not called it a home. Daniel's friend resided with four or five other roommates. Some shared a room together, and some were separated one to a room; it depended on their needs.

Back in the seventies, the disabled were called hostile. I had always taken that name "hostile" to offense. What kind of label is that to put upon our disabled? This gave people the impression that the disabled were confrontational, and that made the public very leery. That couldn't be further from the truth, especially because my son and the majority of the disabled were loving, caring human beings. As time went on, the next choice of name was client, and then finally it changed to consumers. This change was finally made from a direct result of votes based on the input of the mentally and physically challenged.

In the 1980s while Daniel was thriving in his day program, his social worker, who had been in contact with me since he was five years old, believed I should consider putting him on a waiting list for a group home setting now that he was getting older. I was adamantly against this, and my daughter was beside herself at the thought of it. We were always involved in Daniel's day treatment program activities, teaching progress, physical therapy, and family meetings. I considered myself a very involved parent and advocate. It was hard to imagine our involvement in Daniel's life being any other way. The social worker continued to inform me that putting my son on the list would be like having a security blanket. I would not have to use this at all, but in case something happened to me while he was growing up, it would be there. With much hesitation, I opted to listen to her advice. I was also informed the waiting list was long, and if I decided not to add him on and an emergency came up one day, Daniel would be on the bottom.

Eight years passed since Daniel was put on the group home waiting list. He was now twenty-four years and expressed a very strong interest in joining an adult group home setting like his best friend. I tried to push that idea out of his mind and considered it to be a phase. As time passed, it became more evident that his wish to join a group home was not going away. I expressed to the social worker that I would leave the option open for discussion only when I was ready. Daniel's best friend had long since made his move from his group home with Catholic Charities to a group home that was connected to his day program.

Daniel continued to ask me about the group home, adding that he wanted very much to move like his best friend, I continued to put it off by saying I would look into it, but truthfully I was dead set against it. I loved having my son home with me and the family. His friends would come to visit on special occasions. We all unconditionally loved and respected each other.

Chapter 17

Daniel's Wish

ONE DAY THE social worker approached me regarding an agency that was coming to Daniel's program to interview several consumers. They were looking for six candidates to join a group home that they were going to open in Brooklyn. I didn't think much of it, and several days later she approached me on the outcome of the interviews. I was informed that they really enjoyed spending time talking with my son and thought he would be a great candidate. I informed the social worker that I had no intentions of having him go to any group home, especially one run by a different agency. If my son was ever to join, it would be with the same agency he had been with since he had started his day program in 1970. She continued to reassure me that there would be no harm in keeping an open mind, and I should take a look at it because Daniel was older and was interested in having a chance to be like many of his friends.

After much hesitation, I agreed to take a tour of the group home, mostly to satisfy my son. I was impressed with their project and the layout of the home, but not with its location. I set up my son for a visit, but in my gut I was uneasy. I could not imagine him leaving home and not living with our family, but I had taken into consideration his desire to be like his best friend. As a few more meetings went by, I kept in my head that this was really not going to happen, and I could always pull out. I was still hoping for Daniel to move within his own agency that was connected to his day program.

Weeks went by, and I did not hear anything, so I called the agency to ask what was going on. They informed me that they were still moving forward. I now needed to reach out to the executive director, who was the head of the agency Daniel was attending, to ask him what was going on with the progress of the group home situation. I was unsuccessful in reaching him. In the past I had never had any cause to connect with him; my connections were always through the social workers, teachers, and program directors through the organization.

A few more months passed, and I received a letter stating that a meeting was being set up to discuss why the group home was being delayed. Several other parents and I came to the table to hear their concerns, and we were informed the delays were due to financial problems, but their plan was still to move ahead. After the meeting, I figured I would corner the executive director; for the purpose of this story, I will call him Mr. Untouchable. I needed to talk to him about Daniel possibly joining a group home with the same agency connected to his day treatment program. After all, Mr. Untouchable was their executive director and was well aware I wanted to hook up with him. Well, it did not happen. He ducked out after he munched on some donuts and coffee. I should say, he ran out!

Weeks passed again, and by now I was convinced that I was not going to move my son even if the move went forward, because I was not comfortable with him leaving the family with all the negativity going on. The news came shortly after that the group home burnt down, and word was it was of a suspicious origin and involving the agency. This only validated my prior gut feeling that this move would not be a good one for my son. When I informed Daniel the move was not going to happen, he was very upset. I promised him I would look at other avenues to see if I could find something else this time inside his current agency. I continued to try to contact Mr.

Untouchable to pursue my son's wishes, but time and time again I was unsuccessful. I was known in the agency to be a very involved parent, although by no means was I a troublemaker. I was simply a voice when it came to expressing Daniel's needs; I was his advocate.

Now the time had come that I needed to reach out to Mr. Untouchable to talk personally about my son, who was one of the first consumers enrolled in this program. I wanted to discuss the fact that Daniel had been on the waiting list since sixteen, and now eight years later, wanted to join. I wanted to know why he was still waiting and was hell-bent on finding out. My efforts were fruitless, and I was informed by staff that Mr. Untouchable was getting his feathers ruffled by me asking to meet with him. He preferred to have consumers without much family involvement so he could run the agency his way, without interference. I then wrote a letter to the president of the agency, who was also the founder with his partner over seventy-five years prior. Although I had never had the privilege of meeting with him, I have heard nothing but kind, caring words. He also had his two sons involved in the agency. By the time I was able to reach him by letter, he was too sick to follow up with me, so he handed it over to Mr. Untouchable, who was a man with an attitude. I was informed by the organization not to go up against him. He was considered a bully with a temper. In order for me to pursue Daniel's wishes to attend the group home setting with his friends, I had no other choice but to continue my efforts to contact this man, because he was the person who ran the show in the administration. The reality of my pursuing a group home was the start of a long, hard, painful journey that became my family's nightmare.

> *God Blesses those who hunger and thirst for justice, for they will be satisfied. (Matthew 5:6)*

With my husband's encouragement, I began to strongly express Daniel's wishes. I did not want to create any problems or enter a boxing ring with anyone in the administration. Months went by, and I continued to get nowhere concerning the group home issue. I was quite aware by now of the group homes that were opening and were going to be built. Now I was informed by the organization all my correspondence to the agency concerning Mr. Untouchable went directly back to him, including my concerns on his horrible behavior. This lit the fire in my direction for his anger toward me. One man with all the power.

The Lord has heard my plea, the Lord will answer my prayer. May all my enemies be disgraced and terrified. May they suddenly turn back in shame. (Psalm 6:10)

The days turned into weeks, and weeks turned into months. Then with the help of my husband, I did some research on who did the funding on these group homes. First I believed it was the agency my son was attending, but I found out it was funded by the state and charities. I was not naive by any means. My lack of knowledge was due to the fact my son lived at home, and I had no prior experience with group homes and how they were funded. All I knew now was he wanted to join with his friends. This was when I decided to go to the State Department. The office was located in downtown Brooklyn. I needed to go there, so I asked my husband to drive me. I brought a can of Diet Coke and a small bag of chips with me, and off we went. I reached the state building, and the office was on the third floor. I went in unannounced with no appointment; I simply hoped I could talk to someone who was involved with the funding of these group homes. My husband stayed in the car and waited patiently.

The woman at the desk asked me if she could help, and I replied I needed to see someone who overlooked the group home funding. I gave her my name. I believe she felt my anxiety, and she asked me to wait a few minutes then she left the room. Several minutes passed, and the woman came back and told me to go in the office across the hall. When I went into the room, there stood a tall, handsome, distinguished man who looked very kind. He asked me to take a seat, and I did. He asked me why I was there, and I explained my concerns on the group home issue. I told him all about Daniel, his program, his desire to join a group home setting, and the group home that had burned down. I explained how Mr. Untouchable would not answer my calls and ignored me every time I tried to reach him. I wanted to know why.

To my surprise, the man informed me he knew Mr. Untouchable well, and he stated he had no problem contacting him. He walked over to the phone, made a call, and asked to be connected to him. After a short time, he hung up and stated to me there was an opening in New York City for my son in a group home setting. It is sad that one call from someone who held the purse strings was successful, but I, the mother of an active consumer in the organization for nearly twenty years, could not get the respect of a reply. I was very grateful to the distinguished man from the State Department. We talked a little more, and then he told me I would be hearing from the administration very soon. We said our good-byes, I left that day with more questions than answers.

Several days went by, and I received a call from my son's day treatment program. It was a social worker, but not the one with whom I usually deal with. She was told to inform me of the group home that had an opening, and she wanted to set up a date so I could take a look at it. I agreed, although I must say the few days after the meeting, I was very conflicted about it. I was very grateful for the distinguished man's help, but I was working on mixed emotions as to why I needed to go this route in the first place. Why was I shut out by Mr. Untouchable for so long? It was his way of telling me Daniel would not get what he wished for, because I had stepped on his toes.

I wanted to explore more group home avenues to see if they would benefit Daniel, who was also happy in his Brooklyn day program. The agency knew Daniel well, and I felt more comfortable having him in one of their group homes in Brooklyn not New York City. After all, he had been in Brooklyn since he was five years old. I was also not informed that my son was told about the opening in New York City without speaking with me first. I don't believe they meant any harm by telling him, but they should have run it by me first just in the case it was not going to work out. It would be another disappointment for him if I declined.

Daniel and I had such a close relationship, and he loved his family so much that his excitement to move out of our home was hard for me to deal with. Part of what my son wanted to do was what every growing adult wanted, and that was to have some of his own independence.

The Righteous person faces many troubles, but the lord comes to the rescue each time. For the lord protects the bones of the righteous, not one of them is broken! Calamity will surely overtake the wicked and those who hate the righteous will be punished. (Psalm 34:19–21)

Daniel was in his day program on the day of my appointment to see the group home. My daughter was now nineteen, working, and attending college. My husband was still working as a police officer, and I was becoming more anxious by the day. After I went to the program to meet the social worker, the plan was that my daughter would drive us to the city. She did not want to go because she did not want her brother to leave in the first place, so she declined. I drove to the residence with the social worker. Daniel was to stay in his day program so I could look over the apartment that was available and ask questions without him being involved. I did not want him to pick up on any negative feelings I have about the move.

We arrived at the residence in New York City, where Mr. Untouchable had said an opening was available. It was a tall building on a dead-end street backed up to another apartment complex. Many of the tenants were sitting outside. I found out later most of the floors were for senior citizens. I had no idea what was going to be in store for me to see. As we approached the inside entrance, there was a security guard on the main floor we had to pass to enter the elevator. The residence we were to see was on the third floor. It was not the place that I had envisioned my son to be at, especially after looking into other group homes.

We entered the elevator and went to the third floor. We came off and were approached by a nurse. The social worker talked briefly with her, and I introduced myself. Then we continued to Apartment 3G, which was empty. It was a studio with a front balcony. From the very start, I was concerned. The apartment was previously housed by a wheelchair-bound consumer who was moved to a nursing facility. The agency rented the entire third floor of the building. The apartment did not have full accessibility to the bathroom or kitchen to be maneuvered with a wheelchair. The floor tiles were broken, and the place looked like it had not been painted for years. There were exposed wires and broken door knobs with the metal hinges hanging off.

I voiced my opinion and was very concerned about the whole outlook of the apartment. I was visually upset and kept rattling off my concerns. I truthfully wanted to run out. I felt very depressed at that moment. Dealing with the prospect of my son wanting to move out of our home was hard enough, and I had never envisioned the place would look like this. It was especially disheartening. This was coming from a well-known agency, and I was baffled by it all. The social worker tried to reassure me of the changes that would be made before my son would take up residence, but I wanted to leave immediately. We left, and I went back to Daniel's program. I rode home with my son in the van many times before when I had an appointment with staff or to celebrate a special occasion. All the way home, I kept quiet so that he wouldn't catch on to my disappointment of the day's event, he was great at picking up bad vibes, especially with me.

A few days went by, and I received a phone call at home. To my amazement, it was from Mr. Untouchable. He started yelling at me and asked who I thought I was, calling his group home residence a dump. I tried explaining to him over his ranting that I did not call the place a dump, but I could not calm him down. He told me I had a few days to make a decision, or else he would give the apartment to someone else, and Daniel would be out of luck. Before he hung up, he stated to me loud and clear that I should never again step on his toes.

O LORD, keep me out of the hands of the wicked. Protect me from those who are violent, for they are plotting against me. (Psalm 130:4)

Remember your promise to me, "It is my only hope. Your promise revives me," He comforts me in all my troubles. The proud hold me in utter contempt, but I do not turn away from your instructions. (Psalm 119: 49-51)

The next day I called the State Department to talk to the secretary and explain my situation. She connected me to a woman; I do not recall her name. I explained to the woman the situation concerning my call from Mr. Untouchable and the time frame he gave me, with only a few days to make a decision. The woman informed me the state funded the residence. She told me I could take a few more weeks to think about it, and I didn't need to worry about Mr. Untouchable's idle threat.

A few days passed, and I received a call from the head director who oversees all the group home residences. She wanted to meet up with me. This was a woman I had never met before, but I agreed to meet with her. The first time we talked, she was very receptive to my concerns. After we talked about the events that had led me to this group home search, she addressed the issue of the social worker who came with me to my first interview. She believed the social worker did not mean any harm in reporting back to Mr. Untouchable. She believed he would have taken anything she reported to him as an insult no matter how she said it. He was already unhappy with me for going over his head. She told me not to allow him to intimidate me like he had done to so many other parents, staff, and consumers.

The director and I went to the apartment Mr. Untouchable wanted Daniel to move into. I was able to voice my many concerns about the accessibility to the bathroom and the overall condition. The fact was the kitchen was too small to even have my son maneuver to the refrigerator. The place was not equipped for a wheelchair. The director assured me that the apartment would be completely cleaned up, and modified for his needs. All my concerns would be addressed when my son took up residence. While we talked, I was able to meet with some staff and consumers. There were approximately sixteen apartments on the floor. There was a dining room, sit-down area, a living room, and a kitchen. All the consumers had dinner in the dining area. It looked to me that the place needed a complete overhaul. It was certainly a handyman's special and then some.

I was reassured again by the director if I moved in Daniel, all my concerns would be met. She stated it was easier to meet the concerns of these issues while he was in the system rather than out of it. It was quite far from the school program, which meant we would have to change to New York City from Brooklyn, and I did not want that to happen. There was so much to take in. I spent quite a while with the director asking questions and wondering why my son could not move into one of the group homes that were already opened, or one of the new ones being built. It was explained to me that if I moved my son in the residence, and we were not happy, it would be easy to have him transferred. I was told we simply needed to get our foot in the door. I now had to go home and think everything over. I realized I could not take too long because the spot would eventually be taken by another consumer.

I was still bothered by Mr. Untouchable's phone call. Little did I know then that my going over his head to the state would cost my son dearly, along with my family. The saying "You can't go back and change things" is so true. If I could, I never would have considered moving my son out of our home. I did not know then that the administration would use my son as a pawn to get back at me.

Silence their lying lips—those proud and arrogant lips that accuse the Godly (Psalm 31:18)

From the start of Daniel's group home journey, whenever I had concerns, I would contact the Secretary at the residence, her role was a far cry from what a normal secretary does. I immediately felt a connection. It was evident she was a caring person. She explained she had been there for many years and was very involved with the consumers and their quality of care. I was also able to meet with the case manager and director, who were also very pleasant. In the midst of introductions, I was again able to spend a short time with the nurse who overlooked the consumers. I did not have that same welcoming feeling with her as I had on my first visit. There was so much to take in for this move. Would it be right for my son? I had so many concerns questions and fears.

I wanted the right decision to be made for my son's move to the residence because I was filled with so many mixed emotions, and letting go was the biggest one. Daniel wanted this very much, and I wanted to make him happy. My daughter was still against even considering her brother moving out, and my husband left the decision to me. Although I made the final decisions when it came to my son's welfare, I could have used an extra ear to bounce ideas off of. I don't want to call it a cop-out on his part, but I did consider it to be one at that time. Decisions, decisions—that was what every aspect of my life became as a mother. That was when my mom's saying would come back to haunt me: "From the cradle to the grave." Boy, how that was becoming a reality.

I remember sitting down with my son and talking to him about his wanting to be with his friends who had already joined the group homes. I was thinking about how badly he wanted it, and I did not want him to be disappointed by not going. Then I thought as long as I was alive and in his life, I would make sure he was safe and happy, watch him flourish, and still have my son in my life at the same time.

> *But Jesus called them together and said, "You know that the rulers of this world Lord it over their people, and officials flaunt their authority over those under them. But among you it will be different. Whoever wants to be a leader among you must be your servant, and whoever wants to be first among you must become your slave. For even the son of man came not be served but to serve others and to give his life as a ransom for many." (Matthew 20:25–28)*

Chapter 18

The Final Decision

THE DECISION WAS made: Daniel was moving. I wanted to make another visit to look around and meet the consumers and staff, to feel it out again. I remember going up alone, and before I had even started to explore, the nurse who had been there approximately ten years approached me for the third time. She was very to the point in informing me the residence was not suited for my son. That was a far cry from what I was hearing from the social worker, the director of residences, and others! I was quite taken aback by that remark, but I continued to explore.

A few days later, the director asked me to meet her again so we could go over a few more details. I was looking forward to it, especially because I wanted to discuss with her the remarks that were made to me by the nurse. I told the director the nurse had stated she did not think Daniel would be a good fit for this residence. The director told me the nurse was too comfortable in her position and was used to running things without interference or involvement from family members. She believed it would be a great change to have someone like my son to bring in fresh ideas and new life into the residence. She believed the staff was too comfortable in their positions, interfering with the quality of care they were giving the consumers. The administration's mission statement was, "We give the best quality care."

I continued to work with the head director on the move and putting the apartment together. As the weeks went by, I became more familiar with the staff, especially the secretary Mrs. B, who ran the office and did an extraordinary job. She was not only a secretary, she was a godsend to the consumers. I was so happy to have found a comfort zone in knowing she was there for many years and seemed to have so much knowledge and insight concerning the other consumers. Her husband, who was not employed by the agency, was always at the residence, making much needed, necessary repairs to keep it up and running. My son was visiting the group home by now, and he hit it off extremely well with the secretary and the staff, including the case manager. I was promised the changes would be made, and I was confident at that time Daniel would be watched by the twenty-four-hour staff, especially with his activity of daily living care such as showering, toileting, getting dressed, and transferring in and out of bed. That was my top concern in making this move: safety. With all the planning and trying to put things in motion, my husband was trying to stand by me through all my emotions, as well as my daughter's sadness of the brother she loved so much moving out of our home. I told her over and over he would be with us all the time. He would spend weekends with us, and we would visit with him often. No matter how I tried, it was not much comfort to her. I tried to balance my home life while I was focused on my son and his needs, but that never became an issue with my daughter because she unconditionally loved her brother. She was the most loving, unselfish sister a brother could ever ask for.

> *But it was also called Mizpah (which means watchtower)*
> *"For Laban said, May the Lord keep watch between us to*
> *make sure that we keep this covenant when we are out of*
> *each other's sight." (Genesis 31:49)*

I always felt taking care of my son was not a sacrifice but a gift and a privilege. When people would say "Oh, what a burden" or "What a cross you carry," I would become so enraged that they would look at my son in this light. I would tell them that was why God gave me this beautiful boy. This journey was my purpose in life, and having my daughter was also the purpose long before she was ever born. This was in the plan for me. I resented them for their lack of compassion and believed they would not show the same love and commitment to their loved ones that I showed my son. It was for this reason I kept them out of my small circle of friends.

Many years ago, my dear friend Jean voiced to me how much I was blessed. Her young brother, who had just completed his stay in the army a few years before, was killed by his best friend who had a drug addiction. Her brother was trying to help his best friend, and in the process of intervening he lost his own life from being stabbed. The point of this is that back then I was so ridden with guilt over my son's accident that I did not connect why I was so blessed. Now I truly know the meaning. When her mom lost her only son, she was never able to put her arms around him again. Although I had a tragedy, I was able to have my son in my life. I was so blessed, and yes there were times I believed I did not deserve to hear that, but I was so wrong. I know now without any doubt God blessed my son and me by allowing us to be together through the years.

> *Elizabeth gave a glad cry and exclaimed to Mary, "God has blessed you above all women, and your child is blessed. (Luke 1:42)*

Unfortunately, sometimes in my life, I did not see the light through the darkness. On the many different roads I traveled while raising my son, I made choices with so-called friends that hindered my precious time with my children. Although I was always there for them and their needs, so much of my time was taken away to help other people who were not there when I desperately needed their support. For whatever reason, I always gravitated toward the needy people. My husband would call them the vampire friends because they would suck the life out of me. Along my journey with Daniel I experienced feelings of alienation, loneliness, and darkness, from people who deserted me in my hour of need. I was blessed through my faith, hope, and strength to again be able to see my way to the light. I was a woman who always tried to be a happy person, and I always tried to solve everyone's problems while taking care of my family. If I could only go back and regain that time I gave to the vampire friends, I would do it in a heartbeat.

> *For his anger lasts only for a moment, but his favor lasts a lifetime! Weeping may last through the night, but joy comes with the morning. (Psalm 30:5)*

As my gut feeling predicted, the nurse who informed me from the start that my son would not be a good candidate for the group home setting was going to be a problem. She repeatedly harassed me into removing my son, from the residence. Then she tried along with the administration to pass him off as having a behavioral issue. Daniel was well known through the organization as a peacemaker, a gentle giant. Naturally that was not going to sit well with me. I was my son's voice, and I intended to keep it that way, although they would eventually brand me as an interfering mother. I was grateful I had the support of the secretary, who was holding up the fort.

During the first few weeks after Daniel moved in, I was asked not to take him home for any visits, and I should not visit so he could adjust to the new residence. I did not take the administration's advice. I believed from the start my son's move was supposed to be a positive one. Even though he wanted to make this move work like many of his friends had, it was difficult for him to understand he would need an adjustment period. It was going to take time and patience to reach this goal, and that was very stressful for him. Isolating him was not the answer. I did not want to alienate my son from my responsibility of watching over him as his mother.

I already had many fears by allowing my son to make this move. I had wanted to have him reside in Brooklyn in a group home setting—a home, not an apartment in New York. I made this decision based on the promise by the administration that when another opening came up, I would have a fair shot at it. That was not going to be a reality. I did not know this when I entered my son into the residence under these false pretenses, Mr. Untouchable was not going to allow that to happen because I had gone to the state for help and continued to step on his toes.

From the very start of Daniel's arrival at the residence I was already in conflict with the nurse. I was aware she was looking at me as a thorn in her side. She would constantly voice her opinion as to why Daniel did not belong there, saying he was too high functional, which was not true. It was the fact that my strong advocacy for my son interfered with her very comfortable workplace. After all, she was used to being unsupervised; she technically had no boss on-site. Unfortunately, many of the parents for a variety of reasons—death, old age, and abandonment—were not involved, giving the staff free reign to do whatever they wanted. Now here I come along; a healthy, young mother with a voice for my son.

My daughter was still going through a mourning period. She cried, was sad and angry, and was unfocused. She was worried and was basically grieving the loss of her brother not living with the family. My husband went about his business, going back and forth to work and trying to stay out of our way to allow us to work through our feelings. My ex-husband was still living his own life. It was at this time that my daughter reconnected with her biological father. I believed she was looking for additional parental support and guidance that she had not had from him in her growing years, and with her stepdad keeping his distance and my involvement to keep her brother safe, it was very stressful on her. Although she had a great support system from her circle of friends, she desperately sought out moral support from her father since at the time she could not really rely on me for it.

As the weeks passed, Daniel was not eating very well, and I could see he was homesick despite my visiting him and talking to him on the phone every day. I decided to take him home for the weekend. I would have kept him longer, but I did not want to interfere with the adjustment period he was going through. I was trying very hard to allow my son to be aware we were working as a team. The administration asked me again to stay away and not visit or take him home. I told them he was not there for a punishment and said this topic was no longer open for discussion. I asked Daniel when he came home if he still wanted to stay; if not, I would take him back home immediately. Now he was living outside his comfort zone, in the real world. He wanted to stay, and he wanted me to make things better in the residence. Along with his strong desire to stay, he believed I could make it work for him.

The months went by with many issues to deal with on nearly a daily basis in the residence. There were so many problems with staff coming and going, and the residence was a revolving door. Promises were never kept by the administration concerning my son's safety. Unsafe wiring and bathroom issues were not addressed in a safe manner. Every day was a struggle. I was so conflicted. Should I keep him there knowing he could have some independence? Or should I bring him back home to stay?

The long bus ride from New York City to Brooklyn was becoming hard on him. The administration suggested that he may benefit from going to their Manhattan program. That was a big concern for me because he would have to leave his lifelong friends. Now my concerns were multiplying. I started voicing my feelings that I needed to look for a group home back in Brooklyn, which my son and I had wanted from the start. This request fell on deaf ears. Mr. Untouchable was now looking at the secretary at the resident as a big thorn in his side because she was becoming too close to me for his comfort. He was now on a mission to expand the power trip he was already on, and he would make it hard for her to continue working for the consumers' welfare. Eventually she was forced to leave her position that she loved so much because of her constant battles with the administration regarding the safety and happiness of the consumers and my son. I was still going to continue on my journey of relocating him back to Brooklyn to one of the many group homes near me.

Don't put your confidence in powerful people, there is no help
for you there. When they breathe their last breath they return to
the earth, and all their plans die with them. (Psalm 146:3–4)

Daniel's struggles of dealing with his everyday disability and wanting to join a group home in his own agency were tough, but we stuck it out together. The real test came when the administration set out from the start to sabotage his stay. First I was sent to the New York residence, not one in Brooklyn. Then the nurse was plotting with Mr. Untouchable to have me remove my son out of the residence. I was fully committed to my son and to exposing the administration for not being there for Daniel. The administration was horrific in their actions by allowing my son to be in harm's way and have the consumers living in this environment, while brand-new group homes were being built. The more I butted heads indirectly with Mr. Untouchable, the more he tried to stand in my way of making changes for the better. He liked having power to himself, was arrogant in his behaviors, and did not like to be overruled.

You have not taken care of the weak. You have not tended
the sick or bound up the injured. You have not gone looking
for those who have wandered away and are lost. Instead, you
have ruled them with harshness and cruelty. (Ezekiel 34:4)

The nurse continued to voice her opinion about how she felt about my son living in the residence. She resented having my family so involved with Daniel's care because we were interfering with her being able to do whatever she wanted. Technically she was her own boss with no one to answer to—until we showed up. The administration continued to tell me to ignore her. That was very difficult when she would express her feelings every time I came to visit my son. Between me, my husband, my daughter and her friends there was always somebody visiting Daniel. We would clean his apartment, take him out shopping, and go out to eat. We even slept over on many occasions.

It was now five months into my son's move, and we certainly had our ups and downs. He was still trying to adjust and it was taking its toll. One day I received a phone call from the residence director that Daniel was in the hospital. I froze at that moment and then went hysterical; I was back in 1968 again. Fortunately my daughter was home, and she took the phone from me. After what seemed like forever, she hung up and tried to calm me down. My daughter explained to me that Daniel was admitted into the psychiatric ward at the suggestion of the resident nurse. I was beside myself. My daughter asked me to stay home while she went to the hospital with a friend. I promised her I would try to calm down and let her find out what was happening.

Sometime later, she called to inform me the nurse not only told the doctor that Daniel was hearing voices but was experiencing schizophrenic hallucinations. I was devastated. My son was a calm person and had never had such behaviors; this is all documented. I knew right away it was the nurse trying to get him out of the residence, and this was her way of doing it—by telling lies.

Stolen bread taste sweet but it turns to gravel in the mouth.
(Proverbs 20:17)

I was on my way up when my daughter pleaded with me to wait till morning. She was going to stay the night with her brother and stated we needed to wait until the medications wore off. They had Daniel in a lockdown psychiatric unit. There were metal doors that had to be unlocked before she went into his room. There was a guard outside the door to the room, unaware my daughter was behind him, yelling, "Shut up, you retard. Nobody is coming for you. You are never going home."

My boy was strapped down in the bed and so doped up with medication he could hardly talk. He kept saying, "I want to go home." There was no TV in the room, and the outlets were all covered.

Very early the next morning, I left the house to go get my son. If I would have gone to the hospital the night before, they might have put *me* in a locked down room. I was so angry and hurt. There were so many things that I wanted to do to the nurse.

I found out several hours had elapsed before the call was made to my home. The reason why I was now called was because by then the higher-ups in the administration were aware the nurse had made a very bad call by having my son admitted to the hospital psychiatric ward. The head director was very aware of the nurse's negative feelings about my son being in the residence.

> But the cowardly, the unbelieving, the vile, the murderers, the sexually immoral, those who practice magic arts, the idolaters and all liars--they will be consigned to the fiery lake of burning sulfur. This is the second death. (Revelation 21:8)

The resident director apologized over and over for the mistake and assured me it would never happen again. I believe Mr. Untouchable had something to do with the nurse's decision to have my son admitted; she did not act alone. The head director told me the director at the residence should have never agreed to it, especially because he was also aware of the nurse's feelings about my son being there, but she convinced him, and he went along with her decision. I was ready to remove Daniel from the residence and bring him home when I arrived; that was my plan. Before walking through the doors of the psychiatric ward, I put my face to the glass window of the door and looked at my son sitting in his wheelchair in the middle of the hallway corridor. It was heartbreaking. After the guard unlocked the door, I felt very sick and overwhelmed. I walked toward my son.

He was wearing the hospital gown and slippers, and he looked so vulnerable and distraught.

At that moment I felt hatred toward the nurse and the administration for doing this to my son. I wanted to hurt her so bad for doing this horrific act of meanness to him. I was filled with such rage. I walked over to my son and put my arms around him, and we hugged each other. I tried to reassure him he would be okay and this would never happen again. He kept saying, "Ma, I'm sorry," over and over. He was such a good, caring human being. I could not fathom that somebody would do this to him. What a shame to have the person I loved more than life itself be hurt by a professional nurse who was supposed to take care of my son. Instead, she hurt him for her own selfish needs, with the administration's help.

Finally the doctor came in and approached me and my daughter. He shook my hand and stated to me Daniel was fine and should have never been brought to the hospital in the first place. He stated that because of the nurse's insistence he be admitted, they reluctantly did so. The nurse was insisting my son was talking to people and having hallucinations. The medication that day was not administered because of schizophrenia, but because my son was so upset for being taken to the hospital psychiatric ward. When I was signing the documentation to have Daniel released, I noticed the person listed as next of kin on admission was the resident nurse and alongside it was her signature. The doctor informed me that he was going to release Daniel with no signs of any schizophrenia or hallucinations, and he did not need any medication. It was all a mistake.

Oh Lord oppose those that oppose me, fight those who fight against me, put on your armor and take up your shield. Prepare for battle, and come to my aid. (Psalms 35:1-2)

The resident case manager and the head director of residence pleaded with me to not take my son back to my home because of this very bad mistake. The director was very upset, and I believed he was going by what he was told to him by the nurse. I asked my son if he wanted to go back to the residence with me and his sister, where we could talk, or if he wanted to go home. He told us he wanted to go back to the residence. Believe me, in a heartbeat I would have taken him home, but he was okay with going back with all three of us.

> *I am worn out from sobbing, all night I flood my bed with weeping, drenching it with my tears. My vision is blurred by grief,' my eyes are worn out because of all my enemies. (Psalm 6:6–7)*

When we arrived back at the residence, I was informed the nurse had left her job position on her own. I believe it was because she was aware there was no other way out of the horrific situation she had created and she was not alone. Either way, she did not belong back there. My gut feeling was right on about her all along. I thanked God she was not there because if my daughter and I had seen her, I could only imagine what we would have done. To this very day, my daughter cries over what happened to her brother. I never did receive a call or inquiry about my son from anyone in the administration, including the executive director, Mr. Untouchable. I called to talk to him about the incident with Daniel in the hospital, but he never replied back.

> *Yes, I hate them with total hatred, for your enemies are my enemies. (Psalm 139:22)*

The head director asked me to stay strong and not be swayed by the administration ignoring me while I tried to do the right thing for my son. The administration labeled me an interfering parent. The truth was I was a parent, a mother, and an advocate who was looking out for her son's well-being. These were not accidents—they were deliberate acts of cruelty by people who were only there to collect a paycheck. I was doing what a good parent should do: I protected my child. I was not going to allow the administration to intimidate me with what they were doing to achieve their goal, which I believed was to have my son removed from the residence—not because of him, but because of me.

Running a residence took time, effort, and commitment on everyone's part. Being in charge of sixteen consumers, was a tremendous task. My eyes were not blind to that. There were so many problems with one particular consumer. So many incidence's involved him hitting, biting, and spitting at staff, consumers, and visitors. He even punched my daughter on one of our visits. Unfortunately, he created havoc on the part of the consumers. By no means do I blame him for his behavior. I could not believe the administration put consumers who had severe behavior problems with those who did not. I was not made aware of this when my son was entering the residence.

I made another trip to the State Department. I admired the man who had assisted me in finding a group home setting for my son, and I wanted him to know I appreciated him finding an opening, but I needed to express my feelings about this residence and what was conspiring since my son had joined. I also wanted him to be aware of the unfit conditions the consumers were living in and the nurse's involvement in having my son admitted to the psychiatric ward. I told him my son's apartment was clean but only because we kept it up. Only one other consumer had a steady family visitor that was involved in their care. I also said I was not going to stop the fight for my son's safety or the consumers. He agreed but offered no help. I left his office that day with the realization I was in this battle alone to keep my son safe from these bad apples. I never met with the man again. I would always be grateful, but I could have used some much-needed help.

No one who trusts in you will ever be disgraced, but disgrace comes to those who try to deceive others. (Psalm 25:3)

When Daniel lived at home, I was the sole caretaker. I showered him, clothed him, made his food for him, and went on numerous doctor's visits to monitor his health. In the residence they had directors, case managers, secretaries, nurses, social workers, aids, dietitians, cooks, and more. The residence became a revolving door. The staff came and went, it was a confusing situation and a constant battle of egos. Instead of focusing on the consumers, the small dining room area where everyone went to eat was overtaken by the staff's paperwork and battles over who had more seniority over the others.

When my son was having falls, there was no documentation written up on them. Daniel's medical records were never sent from the hospital to the residence. I decided to start recording my phone conversations and gathering documentation to start a paper trail. My thought was if they could do this to my son with his family being so involved, what were they doing to other consumers, especially those who did not have anyone to advocate for them? I was informed by one of the nurses who worked for the administration that Mr. Untouchable believed that we parents should be thankful our child even had beds in which to sleep.

As the years passed, I was still residing in Brooklyn with my husband and daughter, and I was going through so much of my own life's experiences and challenges not only with my son but also with my brother Frank who was diagnosed with Lou Gehrig's disease; he was residing with me and my family.

While I was taking care of my brother at home and Daniel was in the residence, it was the highest stress I had experienced since his car accident. Every challenge that arose was the worst to me at that time, but dealing with keeping my son safe and taking care of my brother was an everyday trial. My brother had been with me for three years, and all that time the administration was giving me grief. I thought hard and with much emotion about bringing my son home, but I did not want him to see my brother going through the stages of his illness.

The administration was very aware of the trials I was experiencing with my brother. I guess I should have not expected them to care about that when they couldn't even address my son's safety issues. The administration was broken, and I resented them. Here was a big agency that had money funded by the state and charities, and they presented themselves as the consumers' heroes. Meanwhile, they could not give my son the safe care he needed, or access for his wheelchair to fit through doorways, or trained staff—but they were still milking the cash cow. While I was attending to my brother and son, I also had a daughter who was basically fending for herself.

Many years ago I met a young attorney that was introduced to me through his father, whom I met while working for my local church taking care of the elderly. One day the young attorney had stated to me, "If you ever need a lawyer, call me." I finally decided to take him up on the offer. I went to his office to have him write letters on my son's behalf to the administration, to have him moved. I felt now was the time to put pressure on these power people. They weren't listening to my pleas when I went to them; it fell on deaf ears. I also needed to show the attorney photos of injuries that my son had received from falls. These were injuries from my son falling out of the shower and off the toilet. This was the bathroom that I had been reassured would be modified. The few frugal attempts that were made to modify the bathroom were a disaster. My husband offered to pay an outside contractor to do the modification, but the administration would not allow it. Again Mr. Untouchable using his power.

By now I was totally drained from trying to keep the residence up to par. In the meantime, the administration received funding and broke down two apartments in the residence to make one big dining room, but they did not do much work to the consumers' rooms. As far as I was concerned, the only ones who were going to benefit from the newly constructed dining room were the staff, and they did. My son still did not have accessibility from his wheelchair to the bathroom. Finally, after more calls and letters to the administration by my attorney, they had some fly-by-night contractor come in and rip out the wall in my son's kitchen to get to the bathroom. That meant my son had to go through the small kitchen to get to the bathroom, leaving it open and exposed to the kitchen area, which was very unsanitary. The roll-in shower they installed let water into the kitchen and living room space, because the shower floor had the wrong pitch. That left my son and staff at higher risk to fall, and they did. It was a slop job, and when they were finished, the dust overwhelmed the entire room.

This was a residence in crisis, and my son and I were continually in the middle of it. After several attempts to look at other residences failed, I went back to my attorney. I also went to the attorney general's office, who was absolutely no help to me. Then I wrote and sent letters to different senators, receiving only one reply. I went to Senator Gentile's office in Brooklyn, and they wrote numerous letters on my son's behalf. I went to my local congressman and councilman, who wrote letters on my son's behalf, to no avail. In the midst of trying these avenues, it was suggested to me to go to an agency in Albany that overlooked the disabled. The investigator came to my home and reviewed all of my documentation, including my audio taped conversations. He was an honest, caring person and had my son's best interest at heart. Unfortunately, when another incident arose, the commission for the disabled would not allow him to handle the incident concerning my son because they felt he was getting too personally involved. They assigned another investigator.

I believe that neither of these agencies wanted me to advocate for my son because it was making waves for all involved. I believe they were working together, and if it wasn't for the caring investigator and all his help, I would not have been able to put together this investigation. The more they bucked me, the harder I tried; the harder they hindered my son's move, the more I was compelled to expose these bad apples.

I had been working tirelessly on having my son relocated back to Brooklyn. I had to go through red tape and phone call after phone call to reach that objective. By now I had audio conversations that entailed abuse, neglect, and cover-ups by the administration and staff. To this day, I have all my documentation and audiotapes in my possession, which will be submitted to the proper people when I am contacted. The investigator deemed the residence to be a circus. He told me no matter what happened and how many hurdles I came up against, I should not stop what I was doing for the safety of my son and the other consumers

After months of an investigation, I was finally able to get my hands on the report. The report showed that the agency was not up to standards and was not giving the quality of care they professed. The report states that my son was left alone on an overnight shift with a staff member who was not assigned to be on that night and had no supervision to oversee him. Then I was informed the man should never have been hired to begin with. One night my son called me crying on the phone because, the same staff member was going ballistic. I then recorded our conversation. The staff member was clearly abusing my son. He also punched him in the head on the side his plate was inserted. He was then fired due to inconsistencies in his story during his interview with police and the agency's in house investigator that showed he was untruthful. This was all in their report. The administration tried hard to keep the findings out of my hands but I did some of my own detective work and was able to retrieve it. When I offered up my audio tape of the incident, the woman investigator did not want to hear it. Why? Because she worked for the same agency where my son was a resident.

It was in my son's best interest that I audio tape these horrific outbursts from staff. I practically lived at the residence, trying to keep the place safe while still taking him back home for weekend visits. I fought to respect his wishes to move him out of the residence and into another group home in Brooklyn. While I was trying to fulfill his wishes, there were so many other issues to deal, such as keeping the place he was in up and running while the administration came up with other settings that were also in unsafe conditions. They had me go to a residence in Brooklyn where his best friend was residing, and I could not believe that they had sent me to a place that was in such dire need of fixing. I came to the conclusion that was exactly why they did it, to discourage me so I would leave the agency.

And we know that God causes everything to work together*
for the good of those who love God and are called according
to his purpose for them. (Romans 8:28)

There were so many other families who were going through similar experiences. Most of them did not want to join me because of the backlash they would receive from going up against the administration; they were afraid that their loved ones would be removed from the agency. It's not that they didn't care—they certainly did, but they were afraid. This was a big agency run by some powerful people, and it had a few bad apples who were in charge and believed they were doing us a favor. There was one family that did take their complaints to the administration, and shortly after their family member who was in a residence was brought to another facility and tied down in bed. The family members were devastated. The father was up in age and worried about his son; his wife had passed, and his children were very concerned about their sibling. These were good people who also went to the commission for the disabled and did not get anywhere. The agency turned their backs on this family whose sibling was being abused.

The power people were working for each other, not for the families. The worst part was they were friends! Mr. Untouchable would have dinner with the same people who were in charge of investigating his agency. How was that for a conflict of interest? It was a joke. They were working for the agency's best interest. I expressed this on many occasions to the commission's office. I had many battles with the head bosses over the investigations, which I had to beg and plead to have the truth put on paper.

But don't just listen to God's word. You must do what it says.
Otherwise, you are only fooling yourselves. (James 1:22)

After the senator's letters and the ongoing investigations, I finally received a call from the new director of residences. It was a female who worked directly under Mr. Untouchable, and she basically did everything he said. Although she was perceived as a very pleasant woman, I had my doubts. To me, she was Mr. Untouchable's gofer. I begged and pleaded with her to have my son moved out of the New York residence. My family and I were, constantly keeping his apartment clean and fixing everything. It was like we were living there and going back to our own home for visits.

While you did all this, I remained silent, and you thought I
didn't care. But now I will rebuke you, listing all my charges
against you. (Psalm 50:21)

Finally after much backlash from the investigations and my attorney, she found a residence directly across from my son's day program that he attended in Brooklyn. By now, after a long fight to have Daniel moved, it seemed to be like a dream come true. During the midst of the move we put Daniel back into the Brooklyn program so he could be with the friends he missed so very much. He would no longer have to take the long bus ride from New York to Brooklyn. The problem now was that the consumer who was living in the studio apartment had not moved out, and they were waiting for him to move to a nursing home. I felt so sad for him. It was the same situation that was presented to me when my son moved to the New York residence. After several months, the consumer finally moved out, and then the head director and I were able to get into the apartment and look it over. I was okay with the layout, but again I was not happy with this bathroom either. She agreed that it needed renovations, and again I was promised that it would be made accessible. I stated to her Daniel had more accessibility to public bathrooms than this agency had for the consumers they housed. They had an occupational therapist come in, as well as the superintendent of the building, and all different kinds of people went in and out of the apartment to evaluate it for Daniel's needs. It took months and months of planning, and more and more promises to my son that this was going to be a reality. By now he was frustrated because he had heard these stories before. Promises and more promises. On and on they went and by now he did not believe it was ever going to happen.

After several years of working tirelessly to have my son moved and many months of putting this apartment together to finally become a reality, we came to another standstill. Now the director of residences informed me that the consumers of the Brooklyn residence did not know whether they wanted my son to move in, which I found out later to be lie. (Here we go again.) She tried to reassure me that everything would be okay. I was livid and asked her why she did not tell me this before we told Daniel about the move and months of renovations. It was another obstacle, which was nothing new for me with this administration. I informed the head director I wanted to attend the meeting with the consumers. The next day, I received a call from her informing me that I did not need to go to the meeting because the consumers decided it was okay for him to move in. There never was a meeting. It was another one of Mr. Untouchable's games, trying to show me he was still the boss.

I received word that the pending move was approaching, and I was informed that my son's twenty-four-hour one to one care would have to be submitted to the state for approval. The woman assigned to help me had taken over the distinguished man's position. She was not under the administration's thumb or control. As time went on, we got to know each other. She then made a confession to me over the phone on audio tape that the residence my son had lived in, was a residence in crisis. She informed me she made a special trip to the residence, which was not her normal routine, and herself stated it was in poor condition. She made this visit because she was aware of the backlash that was going on because of the investigations. I was happy that she was able to validate this for my son and the consumers, and I am quite sure Mr. Untouchable was beside himself with anger.

Finally the move was a thumbs-up. We couldn't believe it, and Daniel was very excited about finally leaving. The residence had been there for many years, and it was right across the street from his day treatment program. I also found some level of comfort in knowing there was a police station nearby to watch out for the consumers. After the move was finally made, I was confident now that after the investigations I had opened, the administration would be vigilant in having the changes made in the New York residence for the consumer's needs. I was told by the state I had made a difference, but only time would tell.

The new setup was much different than the setup in New York City. It was a much smaller building, and each apartment had different needs for different consumers. Daniel was to have twenty-four-hour care one on one. Most consumers had staff individually assigned to them, even their own families were hired. There were staff hired who sometimes did not fit the personality of each consumer. In the New York residence when Daniel was assigned certain staff, I often made a point of having a few handpicked by me to be with him as often as they could. There was one who became his favorite. He was a handsome African American man with a beautiful personality, and he had a great rapport with my son. Daniel usually got along with everybody, and when that didn't happen, most people were aware there was something wrong with the staff member. Everyone knew my son to be truthful. He did not know how to tell lies. He was an honest, caring person who always looked for the best in people—unless someone tried to hurt him, and then he would go to bat for himself. He was certainly no pushover.

Daniel had a second favorite staff member, she was an African American woman who had a day job but had taken this job as a second position for extra income. Daniel loved her, and that meant so much to my family. I wanted these two handpicked staff to come over from New York to Brooklyn. The staff members wanted to come over as well because they loved working with my son. The administration did not want that to happen. I was adamant and discussed this with the head director, the manager, and residence director, stating that they still needed to keep a careful eye open. Although the staff were good people, they had a tendency to play when the cats were away. When staff became too comfortable, they took advantage of that. That was the nature of the beast. Although the head director believed that this would never happen in her residence, she listened to my concerns. I always voiced to the administration that I did not know they each had a crystal ball in their homes. They all seemed to know what was conspiring in these residences when they were not present. I was adamant that the staff be closely watched, especially on the overnight shift, because there was no director or manager in the building at that time. Staff has a habit of making their own rules when they were not being directly supervised, and they were often not properly trained for emergency situations. If one arose, they had to reach out to the director on call, but the director was not always available even though it was mandatory. I wanted my son to make the move with some of the staff he had bonded with over the years; most of all, he cared about them. The head director still wanted to have new staff, but I was very concerned about him being around people whom he was not comfortable with on this new move, so I continued to insist that I wanted these two staff members.

Chapter 19

The New Journey

JUNE WAS HERE, and the move was finally made. After several weeks of Daniel settling in his new residence, I felt like a big load was taken off my shoulders. I wanted to believe this could be the charm for my son. I met with the director of the residence along with the manager. I believed that these two women had my son's best interests at heart and were very committed. I had known the director for quite a few years because she had filled in at my son's prior residence several times. Although she tried very hard, she had a big burden on her shoulders to keep the place safe for the consumers.

Now that I secured the two staff members my son wanted, there were a few other new staff members who needed to be hired. One of them was a deacon. It wasn't too long before my son informed me that while the deacon was watching TV on the overnight shift, he would put a video tape into his VHS machine to watch pornography. He came to work with his little black bag, which I had witnessed on several occasions. That was where he kept his videotapes. I brought this issue to the attention of the director, the manager, and the head director of residences. They tried to persuade me into thinking that was not happening; they told me that wasn't possible because he was a deacon. I expressed to them even deacons and priests could hide behind the cloth—no one was excluded from sinful acts. I said I never wanted him working with my son ever again.

There was another staff member, a woman who Daniel said was not nice to him when they were alone. I expressed these issues to management. Shortly after I voiced this complaint, the manager stated to me that the same staff member complained that Daniel had inappropriately approached her. I realized she was going to say something because of my complaint, but I never fathomed she would say my son had tried to be inappropriate to her. The staff member also told management even though he tried to touch her, she was still willing to work with him. I told management, "I don't think so."

Daniel was not even in this residence a month, and already he was experiencing problems. He was extremely upset that he was being accused of something so ludicrous. In this scenario, we have a staff member who walks around, and a consumer who's wheelchair-bound and cannot walk. Although this staff member stated that my son is being inappropriate with her, she was still willing to work with him. The whole situation did not deserve a response. I would not let her work with him ever again. In Daniel's prior residence, most of the staff would congregate in the dining room while many of the consumers fended for themselves. There was a staff member who tied up one of the consumers in his bed. Instead of terminating her, what did the administration do? They shipped her off to another residence. That was how the administration dealt with the problems: they covered them up.

How long will you people ruin my reputation? How long will you make groundless accusations? How long will you continue your lies? You can be sure of this, the lord set apart the godly for himself. The lord will answer when I call. (Psalm 4:2–3)

It was now July, one month into the move. The woman staff member who came over from New York was doing the 3:00–11:00

p.m. shift, and the male was doing the overnight shift, 11:00 p.m. to 7:00 a.m. I talked to my son every day. We talked in the morning before program, when he came home from program around 3:30 p.m., and in the evening before he went to bed. Then I would get the staff on the phone and talk to them for a few minutes to check on the events of the evening. I would call when the second shift came in because I had so many problems in the prior residence, with staff leaving Daniel for long periods of time. When he used the bathroom, sometimes he would sit there so long he would make the transfer to his wheelchair on his own; this left him at great risk for falls. He was also left in the shower for long periods. It was a constant battle every day to make sure he did not get hurt. The bathroom transfers were a major problem with my son's safety, and this was allegedly with twenty-four-hour staffing. Staff would continually have an excuse that they were using the restroom or were doing the laundry, when in reality they were in the dining room conversing with each other. I was on the phone so much I could have invested stock in the phone company.

Many times Daniel would try to cover for staff because they asked him to do so, and he did not want to get anyone in trouble. I tried not to bombard my son with too many questions, it would only make it harder for him. Daniel was known for his honesty and would cover up for them because he truly cared. I did understand the logic as to why he covered up for them, but I was saddened as to the reason he needed to do it. I would say it was an act of loyalty on his part, but deceit on theirs by using an innocent, caring soul to cover up deception. (Definition of a white lie from the Merriam-Webster Dictionary is - A harmless or trivial lie, especially one told to avoid hurting someone's feelings.)

I will sing of the LORD's unfailing love forever! Young and old will hear of your faithfulness. Your unfailing love will last forever. Your faithfulness is as enduring as the heavens. (Psalm 89:1–2)

One night, I called my son like I did every night before he went to bed. It was about 10:45 p.m. He answered the phone. I said hello and asked him how he was doing, and he said okay. Then I asked him to let me talk to the woman staff member who was doing the 3:00–11:00 p.m. shift; she was one of the two staff members I had requested to come over from my son's previous residence. He said she was not there, and he was all alone. While I was talking to him on the phone for almost thirty-five minutes, the manager then walked into his apartment, and I could clearly hear her asking my son where the staff member was. Daniel said the woman had left and the next person had not come in. It was about 11:20 p.m. By now I was audio taping my conversation because it had become a ritual for me. I asked to talk to the manager, and she was very upset. She came on the phone and apologized over and over for Daniel being left alone. I told her I was thankful she had taken me up on my suggestion to make evening spot checks. Although I cared for these two staff members, I was aware that they had much more freedom in this residence because of the setup. There was no supervision to oversee them during the overnight hours. The manager assured me when the staff member arrived, she would remain the rest of the night and send him home. He wound up coming in at 1:20 in the morning with the excuse that he was stuck in traffic. This meant if I had not called to check on Daniel, and if the manager had not done her spot check, Daniel would have been left alone for several hours. If he went to the bathroom, which he needed assistance with, he could have fallen and had a fatal outcome. Unfortunately, these two staff members were playing games and leaving my son in harm's way, which could have ended tragically.

Very early the next morning, I called to talk to the manager. When I reached her she tried to give me the rush treatment but I was not having any of it. I realized by now, the administration had advised her not to allow me to have too much information on the incident, although I already had it all on audio tape. I pressed on for answers. First she blamed the staff for their lack of responsibility, then she tried to put the blame on me for bringing these two staff members over. Soon after she apologized to me. She was aware it was not my doing. She did not want to directly blame the administration because she needed her job. I felt she was a caring person and genuinely concerned for my son and the other consumers. I was in no way blaming this woman for Daniel being left alone. It fell on the administration and agency.

Daniel was set up to receive a twenty-four-hour one to one. This was especially important because staff was not making rounds here. It was a much different setup then he previously had. The protocol for the prior residence was to have staff members rotate from room to room. That was not going to work because Daniel was at risk for falls. I talked to the staff member personally and confronted her as to why she would walk out on Daniel before the next staff member had arrived. She was shocked that he was left alone for all of those hours. I told her if the staff was late relieving her, she was supposed to stay until he came in. She told me she needed to go to her day job and had to go home to sleep. As a result, she was terminated. Of course my son was very sad and disappointed, and so was I. The bottom line is she did not do the moral thing in caring for my son, so it was in his best interest for her to leave. When the next shift came in at 1:20 a.m., to his surprise he was greeted by the manager, not the staff member. They might have been playing games, but I certainly was not. I believed he was also going to be terminated, but the administration informed me that he was going to be on probation. Although they were aware of his not being truthful about being delayed in traffic, they said they could not prove if he was making up the story, and the previous shift should have never left until he arrived. I was informed he was still going to work with my son. I was very disappointed by now and did not believe in him as I once had.

Two months into the new move, I was in New Jersey at my daughter's house, staying for a few days to watch her home while she went away with her family. Around 12:15 a.m. the phone rang, and I was startled out of my sleep. It was the staff member who had been put on probation for arriving late. By instinct, I hit the record button. I knew right away it was bad news because that was how I now lived my days. I was always worried. "What is wrong?" I asked him. He told me Daniel wanted to get something to eat and buy Diet Pepsi. I answered, "Okay, why?" I was still groggy from being woken up and was not thinking clearly. He told me he could not leave him alone, so he had taken him out. He then informed me on the way home from the corner deli, he had brought two or more cups of very hot coffee and placed them on top of Daniel's lap while walking him in his wheelchair. The coffee had burst open all over Daniel's stomach. I asked him why he bought the coffee, and he said some of the other consumers in the building had asked him to do it. He kept repeating he could not leave Daniel alone—I guess he was trying to prove a point to me. My son had been getting ready for bed when I talked to him earlier, and he had plenty of Diet Pepsi in his kitchen closet. I realized that the staff was trying to cover up and make excuses for taking him out. The office and I always made sure Daniel had plenty of Diet Pepsi. After all, he was well known as the Pepsi Man. The staff member proceeded to tell me my son was okay, and he only had some small bubbles in the middle of his stomach. He then stated to me he had put water on it. I tried very hard to stay calm and told him to put my son on the phone.

Daniel came on the phone right away. I asked him to please tell me how he was. He said he was okay, but he would always say he was okay. He then proceeded to tell me what had happened. I was very skeptical due to the incident the month before. Daniel was not covering up for him this time, then I asked him to let me talk to the staff member. I then asked the staff if he contacted the director on call, and he said yes. The director told him not to call an ambulance; she said to play it by ear. Her advice to him should have been to call an ambulance immediately and let them assess Daniel's burns, not the staff.

The director on call needed to be reached at her house phone because she did not have a cell. The administration would not give her one, which was mandatory. It took several minutes for me to get her number because the staff member needed to find it again. When he found it, he gave it to me. I called her to discuss the incident that had just occurred, and she stated to me she informed the staff to keep watch on the burns. By now I was more than livid and it had been hours since my son had been burnt. I called the staff member back and asked him how Daniel's stomach looked. He said it wasn't bad, just a few more bubbles popping up. I did not believe him and told him to call an ambulance immediately.

He told me he called for a van, but there were none available. I yelled, "Call 911!" Then he stated he could not find Daniel's medical card; he believed it was downstairs in the office. I shouted at him to call an ambulance and tell the security to open the office downstairs so he could access the medical card. It was chaos, with phone calls back and forth. The ambulance eventually took my son to the emergency room, where he was treated for second-degree burns.

I called the director back to tell her what was going on, and she informed me that she talked to the staff and could not believe the he had taken Daniel out when she was well aware that he had all he needed in his apartment including his Diet Pepsi. She told me the staff was not telling the truth. Later on during the investigation, she recanted her story and said Daniel needed to get something to eat and drink. Although the director recanted her story and the investigator was aware of the audiotape being validated they did not put this in the report. That is why I did not have any faith in the Albany-based agency that sugar-coated everything, so they could continue to allow the administration to go unscathed from any blame. This director was one of the good apples who was simply just trying to protect her job position which was her bread and butter for her family. I believe she truly cared about my son. This director also worked at my son's prior residence. Although at the time it was very disheartening to me that she herself told a white lie. I was aware of why she recanted her story: for fear of the backlash she would receive from the administration, especially Mr. Untouchable. I did not push the evidence concerning the audio tape for fear of her losing her job.

I talked to my son when he returned from the ER hours later, and I reassured him I would be there early in the morning. I instructed the staff to keep him home from program the next day. The next morning I called early to make sure the medication was being applied to Daniel's burns. The staff informed me he needed to have the prescription filled, so he was going to go over to the program to have the nurse apply the medication. I had already made up my mind before Daniel moved that if any other incident happened to my son, I was going to take him back home. I would be thankful to God that he didn't come out of the residence in a body bag. I considered my son and I to be so blessed that he wasn't fatally injured, I called the program nurse. She calmed me down and told me that they would get the prescription filled, because neither the director nor the manager were not in the office, and they would not be until 9:00 a.m. I informed the nurse I would be there very soon. She stated to me she looked at Daniel's burns and was shocked they were second-degree. She stated it looked so awful.

I arrived at my son's residence as soon as possible and was devastated by his injury and the fact that he sat there for several hours before going to the emergency room. All this while everyone was running around and making decisions without even knowing what my son had endured! After all the events that had transpired, the only one who called to check on my son's condition was the director, whom I had spoken with the previous evening. I reached out to the head director, who was now on vacation, and she did not answer. She informed me if I ever needed to talk to her for any reason, her cell phone was universal. She did not pick up. Finally when I did reach her, she stated to me she was sorry I could not reach her, adding there must have been something wrong with her cell phone. I did not believe that for a moment.

By now the Commission for the Disabled wanted to get rid of me, but there was still the honest investigator who was in my son's corner. I called the investigator to talk with him about the burn incident, and I was informed another investigation needed to be opened. I tried to reach his boss, but he would not give me the time of the day. I recall during the first investigation, I had to plead with them to put in the report what the investigation had found. The investigator informed me some of his findings were not allowed to go into the report; he was told to edit it by his bosses. I always believed the commission was there only because of the squeaky wheel I had become. I would have never been able to get as far as I did if I wasn't the squeaky wheel—and even that was not far enough.

The obstacles that kept Daniel and other consumers in harm's way were an uphill climb that became a mountain. That mountain was created by these two agencies that were allegedly there to protect the disabled. The people who donate funds to these agencies do not realize what really goes on behind closed doors. People who gave their money and volunteer time needed to look at where it was going, not just the surface. They also needed to explore the abuse and neglect statistics, as well as the allegations made by the parents, consumers, and advocates. They needed the viewpoints from the agencies and organizations to whom they are supplying their funding. This needs to be explored big time, because some of these agencies are wolves in sheep's clothing.

Money is not a voice. We the people are the voice. The freedom of information law enables the public to access copies of performed investigations and their outcomes regarding all allegations of abuse and neglect involving the disabled and the elderly. The problem is the truth is not put in the reports. This may not always be what they are looking for because the real truth can also be camouflaged. I've been there and done that with the state commission for the disabled throughout my son Daniel's investigations, what you see is not always what you get. Unfortunately, the truth will not always prevail. We the people need to dig deeper and deeper for the truth. It is out there—believe me. When Daniel was subjected to being in harms way in his residence, all the investigations were done by the agency's in-house investigators, and these so-called investigations always seemed to come out in the administration's favor.

In my desperation I prayed, and the Lord listened, "He saved me from all my troubles." (Psalm 34:6)

That is why I went to the state commission with my proof and audiotapes. I went to them because I believed they were truly going to be Daniel's knight in shining armor. Although I had a very good experience with my first investigator, the rest of my experience was hell while dealing with these people of power. I was just a common mother who loved her child and wanted the best for him. My only objective was to have Daniel flourish in his group home. This is what any human being would want in his or her life: some independence. In the end, it wasn't about independence; it was about safety and survival with an administration that battled me every step of my way to reach that objective. In the previous residence in New York, staff taking care of my son, along with one of the female consumers, had them undress and put them in bed together to see if they would have sexual contact. I came upon this information because my son told me what conspired when I was not there. When I confronted the staff, they told me the information he gave me was true, but of course it was never written up or investigated. When I explained this to the administration, their answer was, "This doesn't happen in our house." You see whenever I went to the administration with any issue, they always referred to the group homes as "their house." That was part of the problem. It was not their house—it was the consumers' house. They went to their own homes with their fancy cars and took vacations from the money they made off of the consumers, while letting the consumers live in rundown, unsafe facilities. They were making their six-figure salaries from donated money.

I will not allow deceivers to serve in my house, and liars will not stay in my presence. (Psalm 101:7)

When it was finally approaching the end of Daniel's stay at the New York residence, I was handed a letter by another director. The letter stated I could no longer stay overnight and had to notify them when I visited my son. I stayed for numerous days, nights, and weekends, and I took him to the family's home in order to watch over him. There were many times when there was no staff coverage. The manager, secretary, and director had to watch the consumers in the office, which also included Daniel, on several occasions. When the consumers came home from a long day at their program, they wanted to go into their apartments and unwind. There were times when I was at the residence, some of the consumers would stay in the office for hours on end.

The next day the head director called to apologize about the letter and stated it should never have been written. Of course I realized the letter came from the order of Mr. Untouchable. When the letter was delivered to me personally at my son's residence, the director who handed it to me explained he was sorry and did not want to do it, but it was an order given by someone higher up. Being the squeaky wheel that I was, the decision was overturned because I was not standing for it anymore.

If we claim we have no sin, we are fooling ourselves and not living in the truth. But if we confess our sins to him, he is faithful and just to forgive us our sins and to cleanse us from wickedness. (John 18:9)

Chapter 20

Coming Back Home

DANIEL'S BIRTHDAY, AUGUST 24, was approaching, and he was badly burned on August 9. I had plans to go to Wildwood Amusement Park in New Jersey for a three-day adventure. There was a boardwalk with games, rides, and entertainment. The burns were very bad on his stomach, so I was going to cancel our hotel reservations. He was very upset and asked me to please not cancel; he was looking forward to this trip. That was all I needed to hear, so it was a thumbs-up.

A few days later, we arrived and walked for hours on the boardwalk till the wee hours of the morning. There was an artist walking along the boardwalk doing pictures of anyone who wanted to be drawn. Daniel wanted one. The man drew a large sketch of a cartoon character, a lookalike of my son sliding downhill in the snow with a polar bear sitting next to him. He was sliding down holding a can of his favorite drink, Diet Pepsi.

These are the things we did together with so much love. Daniel was always so happy with life. He never drank, smoked, took drugs, or had an intimate sexual relationship. Daniel was intimate with life. His intimacy came along with family, friends, animals, his movies, and music. He unconditionally loved people and his pets. He was so trusting. He loved—and I mean loved—his Diet Pepsi.

I look back at all the mistakes that were made. While my son was residing in his New York residence, he came home for his weekend visit with a lingering cold. He was prescribed an antibiotic. I noticed he was scratching himself. My gut instinct told me something was wrong because he had a little trouble breathing. I checked the antibiotic and could not believe it was penicillin. Daniel was allergic to penicillin! I called the residence and asked to talk with the nurse and asked why he was given penicillin, and whether it was noted in his records. The nurse stated it was. I insisted while I was on the phone that she put it in the alert book that he was sent home with the penicillin. Before I sent Daniel back to the residence, I confirmed with the nurse that it was put in the medical book. I later came to find out no documentation was logged in. Due to this incident, it was uncovered there were no medical records at all for my son at the residence because they were never sent over when I signed all the release papers back in 1990.

Reflecting back to when the investigation was going on for my son, it came to light the hospital medical release forms that I signed on all his medical care were never retrieved from the hospital. The first thing I was asked before my son entered the residence was to supply important documents that were required: his birth certificate, social security card, any documentation on health issues, and medical release papers from the hospital at which my son was a patient. I was informed by the administration that the medical records were sent for and that they were locked up in a safe placed in the office. All those years, and they never had any records, but all along they told me they had them!

I had to sign new release forms and constantly keep up with the residence to make sure they were retrieved. When that didn't happen, I had to personally make many phone calls to the hospital to retrieve them myself. When the medical records were finally delivered to the residence, I went there the day they were delivered. I wanted to be there for the sole reason of seeing them. I sat there in the office, went through the medical records, and found all my personal social service information along with the medical records that the residence wanted. I was so upset that all this time that passed, and the administration never had Daniel's medical records. I could not believe how irresponsible they were—but then again, I could believe it, with all the things they had put my son and family through. I have written documentation on this in my investigation report. It came out down the line that a male nurse stated he was asked to change medical records on other consumers by the administration and he refused. He left shortly after. I was not at all surprised.

Daniel came home on another weekend visit with a gash on his back. I discovered it while changing his sweatshirt. It was not covered with any bandage and was quite deep. I asked him how he received the wound, and he told me he was left in the shower for a very long time. When nobody came back to get him out, he transferred himself from the shower to the wheelchair and slipped, causing him to scrape his back on the back of the chair that was missing a rubber casting.

I called the residence immediately, and they informed me they were not aware of the incident. I needed to take photos to show the administration. When the state tried to investigate and retrieve the report, they were told it happened at my home on his weekend visit. Then why was a report not written up when he returned back to the residence with an injury to his back? Because they were well aware it never happened at my home. There was no report written up before he left the residence or after he arrived back. This was another one of their lies. It was not only the staff that was responsible but the administration who did oversee them. I was there to uncover their lies. In fact, The Investigator told me he was shocked that the previous state audits were passed considering the residence was in such poor condition. Although he was shocked, I was not.

> Look at those who are honest and good, for a wonderful future awaits those who love peace. But the rebellious will be destroyed, they have no future. The Lord rescues the godly he is their fortress in times of trouble. The Lord helps them rescuing them from the wicked. He saves them, and they find shelter in him. (Psalm 37:37–40)

At this point I was introduced to another woman from the state department. She was going to be the go-between the administration and me to have Daniel moved. She certainly had her work cut out for her to keep the calm while the storm was brewing. I personally believed the administration did not give a damn because she was taking all the heat off them. This woman was a genuine, decent person working to undo the damage that had been caused to my son and the family. I believed that she was looking out for Daniel's best interest. After Daniel's burn incident, there was no doubt that I was going to take him back home. I had already moved to New Jersey a month before Daniel's move back to the Brooklyn residence. The reason I moved to New Jersey was not only because my daughter resided there, but I made the decision that if it did not work out for my son, I would be prepared to have a proper setup for him to come home. I purchased the house from my daughter and contracted the house to have an addition put on for Daniel, me, and my husband.

This addition was going to be set up for all of Daniel's needs. He would have his own room and a modified bathroom that was accessible for his wheelchair. I discussed with my son about him leaving the group home setting and the reasons why it would be better for him to come back home. He was happy and so wanted to just have a safe environment, which he could not have with the agency. I informed the administration that I was going to remove my son from the agency and also from his thirty year program because our home was now in New Jersey, and it was too far for him to travel every day. It was a very painful decision for me to make because Daniel loved his program so much, but I felt it was the only moral thing to do. I realized as time went by that removing my son from his program was a mistake, but I was so done with the administration that I just wanted to run with him.

My state senator, Vincent Gentile from Brooklyn, was a great advocate for my son, and his staff was wonderful. They wrote so many letters to the administration. There were times that the administration totally ignored his letters, and his office was not going to have any of that. All the documentation that I gave regarding the negligence and abuse that was discovered within the agency was taken into consideration when these letters were written. The senator was also aware that I was severing ties with the agency due to my son's lack of quality of care.

There was a sweet, beautiful woman who lived in the same residence as my son in NYC. After I removed Daniel from the agency, she went out one night in the van with the driver and a staff member. On the way back to the residence that evening, the driver let the staff member off at the bus stop so she could go home early, and that left the driver all alone with the consumer. When he reached the residence and it was time to assist her off the van, he left her by herself on the lift high above the street, and she rolled off and hit her head against the curb. She remained in a coma for several months before she passed away. I had this on audio tape because I still kept in touch with some of the staff after Daniel had left the agency. It was clearly stated that they were doing everything they could to cover it up, and the administration was aware that the staff member was not there to help take her off the lift and assist the driver, and because of this horrific incident, she died. The senator had all of this documented. The bus driver did not even call an ambulance or the police. He simply picked her up, put her in the van, and drove her to the hospital. All this chaos from not knowing what to do and not having staff available for her was the cause of her death.

Warning to the rich. Look here you rich people; Weep and grown with anguish because of all the terrible troubles ahead of you, your wealth is rotting away and your fine clothes are moth eaten rags, your gold and silver have become worthless. The very wealth you were counting on will eat away your flesh like fire. This treasure you have accumulate will stand as evidence against you on the Day of Judgment. You have spent your years on earth in luxury, satisfying your every desire. You have fattened yourselves for the day of slaughter. You have condemned and killed innocent people who do not resist you. (James 5:1, 3, 5–6)

There were so many incidents that were not written up—too many to mention. I went to other sources for help. I went to the attorney general at the time, and his staff wouldn't give me the time of the day. I was a concerned mother with issues involving her son and his safety, and this man was involved with unlawful acts himself. They are no words to explain what kind of people our families have to turn to when we need help. Just look at some of the candidates running for office who are themselves involved in unlawful misconduct. These are the people of power who get adrenaline from the win. They will stop at nothing and have no shame about reaching their goal for that win.

If a doctor was operating on your child and caused injury, and he or she came to you and apologized, would you let the doctor operate again? Would you give them a second chance? What will it take for somebody to realize that this system is badly broken? How many mistakes have to be made before we say enough is enough? With all things that are happening in today's world, the most important is saving our children. There is nothing that is more important than their safety. Doctor Vincent Fontana states, "To save one child's life is to save the world."

Children are a gift from the Lord." They are a reward from him. Children born to a young man are like arrows in a warrior's hands. How joyful is the man whose quiver is full of them! He will not be put to shame when he confronts his accusers at the city gates. (Psalm 127:3, 4,-5)

After removing Daniel from his residence and program, I soon came to the realization I made a very hasty mistake by severing my ties with the agency. I wanted Daniel to move back into his last group home residence—the one I fought so hard for. I was willing to move in with my son and be his full-time caregiver, to allow him to be with his friends. There were families who resided with other consumers and were being reimbursed. I was looking for no financial payback, just my son's happiness. The administration denied my request and informed me I was too late over my thirty-day window to get back in. I was never given this option when I removed my son. A letter was written by my state senator to the administration and to HUD on my behalf, to allow me to reenter the Brooklyn residence and be my son's sole caretaker. It was denied by the agency but not by HUD.

I realized that Daniel missed his friends and needed to go back to his program. I could not see him going through so much pain. He needed his friends and the teachers who were involved with helping him flourish in his lifetime. I contacted the head director to try to get him back in. It was not about my having regrets of my removing him from the agency; it was about him being connected back to his program. I realized the administration was not allowing my son to go back to the group home because they found their solution by outing me when I left. I was not going to pursue any more group home options with the agency, but I needed to get Daniel back in his program. The head director of residences, who was one of the two bad apples, was very open to my son going back because she was now well aware of the chaos that was caused by her and Mr. Untouchable being negligent, allowing my son to be in harm's way due to their deplorable behavior. I was continually on a roller coaster ride, going up and down over and over. After much conversing, the head director came up with a solution of Daniel being picked up in New Jersey and going to Brooklyn. At the time I had no other choice but to give it a try. I wanted very much to try any solution that would take my son out of his mindset of being alienated from his friends, but I was sick thinking of him going back on the van again due to past safety issues. The main reason I wanted Daniel to reside in the new group home across from his program was for safety and to eliminate busing. Now I was starting all over again.

After the van came to pick up my son, I had to go through the rituals of the safety issues. The first day he went to program was mind-boggling, and I worried about him traveling on the highway. This situation could not last long, I was not happy with this so called solution the administration came up with especially do to their past behaviors. I terminated the bus situation and decided that I would have to come up with my own plan. After talking to the lady from the state and explaining to her what was going on, the only solution we came to was for me to get an apartment back in Brooklyn so I could have my son transferred from my apartment to his program. Again Daniel would still have to be bused. All this was so much chaos for Daniel and my family, and it was the direct result of an administration that failed my son.

I found an apartment back in Brooklyn. It was on the sixth floor in an elevator building. The state was willing to fund the apartment and asked the landlord to modify the bathroom for Daniel's needs. I signed a two-year lease, and the state was willing to have me purchase the furniture as a result of all the mistakes that had been made while Daniel was residing in New York, and then Daniel being burned after his move to the Brooklyn residence. They wanted to do everything they could to resolve this horrible mess the administration and the state department, who passed bad audits had put us in. My daughter now had to drive us everywhere. My husband did not drive any longer, so he decided to stay in the Brooklyn apartment. I stopped driving on the highway because by now I was not comfortable getting behind the wheel. This left my daughter with the burden of driving the family back and forth. She also had her own two boys to attend to back home.

I called to talk with the Commission for the Disabled concerning Daniel's burn investigation. I tried to reach the head boss, but he would not give me the time of the day. I recall when the first investigation was being done, I wanted crucial information that was founded by the investigation to be put in the report, but the commission would not hear of it. The investigator tried his best not to edit out important information he believed should be in the report, and again they denied his request. It was obvious the state commission was not looking out for my son or my family.

Shortly after I was settled in the Brooklyn apartment, I was contacted by the Commission for the Disabled to meet with the investigator, who was already investigating the burn incident and wanted to discuss the events that had led up to that night. He came along with a partner. He was not courteous to me and had an attitude from the start. He had also worked on my son's first investigation like a silent partner, and wanted nothing to do with informing me on any updates.

During the interview, the investigator requested he take my original audio tape of the burn incident. I informed him and his partner after they listened to the tape that there was no way I was going to hand over the original. I told him I would make a copy and send it to him. He told me he needed the tape now and said it was going to cost the agency time and money to have the tape transcribed; it would hinder the investigation. I replied, "Sorry, but I am no fool." I believed if I handed over the original audio tape, when the time came to give it back, it would be among the missing items of the report. By now I had no trust in the state commission, especially because the original investigator told me he believed his agency was not doing its job in Daniel's best interest. I was given permission by him to audiotape our conversation, which I also have in my possession.

The lady from the state informed me that as long as I was trying to reach the goal to keep Daniel in his day program, they would continue to do whatever they could to help me by funding my apartment, my furnishings, and the modifications, including widening all of the doorways so Daniel could have access in his wheelchair. Ironically it was not long after that I received a letter from Mr. Untouchable stating he was very happy to welcome Daniel back into the program. I could not believe after all the years I tried to contact this man to keep my son safe, and this bad apple was now willing to correspond with me. I needed to dig deep within myself to find this laughable; if I did not, it would be too painful for me to comprehend the irony of it all. I believe in my heart of hearts that Mr. Untouchable sent me that letter to convey a message to me: "Ha-ha, I won." I was so desperate to have Daniel back in his program that I was not going to allow even his bogus letter to stand in my way.

While Daniel was attending the program, my attorney from New York submitted lawsuit papers to the agency in 2000 involving the abuse and neglect that Daniel had endured while under the administration's care. At that time my attorney informed me that there could be a risk of retaliation against my son by doing this lawsuit.

The Godly will rejoice when they see injustice avenged.
They will wash their feet in the blood of the wicked. Then
at last everyone will say, "There truly is a reward for those
who live for God; surely there is a God who judges justly
here on earth." (Psalms 58:10–11)

Earlier on, I explained to the head director of residences that I would be going to pursue a lawsuit because her agency was never committed to my son's safety. She did not believe me. I had informed her many times that I was going to go to outside help. It had taken me a long time to come to the realization that the administration was never going to comply with my concerns. I was so angry that I believed that they were toying with my son's life. This was a well-known agency and I could not fathom the conditions they were having the consumers live in, along with all the cover-ups that were going on behind closed doors. It was only when the investigations were opened and the lawsuit was filed that the administration came in after Daniel moved out and did the much-needed renovations.

I do not spend time with liars or go along with hypocrites. (Psalm 26:4)

For God watches how people live, he sees everything they do. No darkness is thick enough to hide the wicked from his eyes. We don't set the time when we will come before God in judgment. He brings the mighty to ruin without asking anyone, and he sets up others in their place. He strikes them down because they are wicked, doing it openly for all to see. For they turned away from following him. They have no respect for any of his ways. They cause the poor to cry out catching God's attention. He hears the cries of the needy. (Job 34:21-28)

Unfortunately, my son's best friend was not treated with respect by the administration. I had numerous communications with the director of residences concerning this matter, and it was passed off as this loving soul had behavior problems. This was the administration's scapegoat when an incident occurred that resulted in staff abusing the consumers. I have an audio tape of Daniel's friend crying out to me for help. Down the road, I came to find out that staff member knocked him out of his wheelchair. I was never given the opportunity to have it heard by the state commission in Albany; they were not at all interested in listening to it. I did take it upon myself to make phone calls on this critical issue after my son left the agency. When I brought this up again to the director of residences, she stated to me that the incident involved was due to the consumer's behavior. He was abused. The audio tape does not lie, and I believe the truth will eventually win over. Daniel and his best friend conversed all the time by phone until this incident came up, and then his friend was no longer able to call or have any contact.

Is it because you're so pious that he accuses you and brings
judgment against you? No, it's because of your wickedness!
There's no limit to your sins. The righteous will be happy
to see the wicked destroyed, and the innocent will laugh in
contempt. They will say, "See how our enemies have been
destroyed. The last of them have been consumed in the fire."
(Job 22:4–5, 19–20)

While my lawsuit was moving forward, I received a phone call from my attorney's secretary to update me on the case. Now that Daniel was back home and safe out of the residence, it was time for me to go full speed ahead on bringing these bad apples to the justice system. I cannot count the times I went in and out of my attorney's office to put this case together; by now there were seven standing causes of action against the administration and its agency. The attorneys whom the agency hired initially eventually pulled out when they could not get the court to throw out the case. Then they moved on to another law firm, who eventually also pulled out when they could not reach the objective to have the lawsuit thrown out. This left the insurance company for the agency very frustrated.

There were long periods when we had to wait many months for a decision by the courts to see if my case was still standing, and then the judge's decision would be in my favor, including all audiotapes that were admissible to the court. The agency's insurance attorneys desperately tried to have those audiotapes thrown out but could not make this happen.

Shortly after I moved Daniel and me into the apartment, the lady from the state department stated to me, "No matter how hard it is for you, your relationship with the agency is not a healthy one. You must bite the bullet and move on. You cannot do this to yourself any longer. It is like a severely broken marriage." I realized she was right by what she was saying, but at the time I kept going over what had conspired over the years, and it drove me more to want to fix what was badly broken, and I could not. I then made the decision to take her advice, and with a very heavy heart I removed Daniel from his program for the second time.

My last and final request was to have my son visit with his best friend. Daniel loved this boy, who grew into a great man. The administration would not allow it because they were aware Daniel's best friend was being abused, and I had an audio tape of it and had called several agencies for the disabled to report it. The administration would not allow Daniel and his friend to talk anymore. It was also due to my pending lawsuit against the agency. The organization that ran the day program Daniel had attended tried to set up a visit but received no response. The state tried and failed as well. This was when they encouraged me to continue with the lawsuit and told me the administration deserved what they get. During the battle to try to have my son visit with his best friend, we received news he had passed away. They never did get to reunite. I told my son that his friend loved him very much but had to move away. I could not tell him he had passed.

I went to the funeral, and some of the clan from the administration were there. I paid my respects along with my daughter and left. I did not converse with anyone in the administration, and they made no attempts to converse with me. There were also many consumers who attended. When I went back home, my heart was broken to look at my son face to face and not be able to tell him his best friend had passed I believe if he was told, his grief would have been unbearable.

Turn to me and have mercy, for I am alone and in deep distress. My problems go from bad to worse. Oh, save me from them all! Feel my pain and see my trouble, Forgive all my sins. See how many enemies I have. And how viciously they hate me! Protect me! Rescue my life from them! Do not let me be disgraced for in you I take refuge. May integrity and honesty protect me. For I put my hope in you. (Psalm 25:16-21)

Laughter can conceal a heavy heart, but when the laughter ends, the grief remains. Backsliders get what they deserve; and good people receive their reward. (Proverbs 14:13–14)

Years of hell and back with this administration were finally coming to a close. After two long investigations and hundreds of hours of audio tapes, I could not subject my son or family to any more heartache. My son's safety was my first priority. So many families I encountered over the years whose siblings were being abused stated how afraid they were to go against the administration for fear of retaliation on their loved ones. Look where Daniel ended up: with a journey of broken promises and broken dreams.

But is it wrong to say God doesn't listen, to say the Almighty isn't concerned you say you can't see him, but he will bring justice if you will only wait, you say he does not respond to sinners with anger and is not greatly concerned about wickedness.*But you are talking nonsense Job you are talking like a fool. (Job 35:13–16)

The lady from the state advised me of another program in Brooklyn that I could explore. I was very familiar with this day program, located four blocks from my home I sold and thirty blocks from my new apartment. This program was a good one and had a great history for doing well for the disabled, so she made an appointment for Daniel to see it. The day arrived and even though it was a very cold winter day, I decided to walk there with my son. We had to pass our old house that we shared together for twenty years. I figured the walk in the cold air would do us good, and we could talk on the way. I made sure he was quite bundled up. After we were reaching our halfway mark to the program, we were passing our old home and Daniel wanted to go down the block we shared together for so many great years. I brushed it off, telling him it was too cold.

Here we were now, going back to a place that we no longer shared. Daniel had lost his day program that he attended thirty years with his lifelong friends, and now I was trying to put the pieces of my son's life back together. We finally reached our destination and the lady from the state was already there. This woman was a breath of fresh air and truly cared about doing so much to find a solution to a long-standing problem.

We stayed in the program for a while, and after the interview was over, the conclusion was Daniel would try the program out for a few days. That decision left Daniel very unhappy. It was a very small and structured atmosphere for him, and my heart was breaking. He was heartsick for his program and for his home in Brooklyn. On our way going back to the apartment, we walked approximately four blocks, and Daniel said right away, "Ma, stop." He wanted to go down our old block because he missed it so much. It was a small attached home, but to him, it was a palace where we had great times and great memories. I explained to him it was too cold to go by, so I shuffled my pace to a faster one. I wanted to get back to the apartment as fast as I could. I look back on that day, and of not walking down memory lane with my son so he could see his memory home. I will live with this regret forever.

By now I felt like the whole world was on my shoulders. I had just gone through a bad depression and severed my ties with the agency for the second time, so I could imagine how my son felt. Taking him out of his thirty-year program without thinking that part through put me back on the guilt journey. I was heartbroken over not being able to fulfill his wishes of residing in a safe group home. All in all, my son still put his faith in me. Why did I deserve unconditional love from such a caring loving soul? This growing young man who had weathered so many storms over the years was so amazing that he still trusted me. Wow. I was so blessed that this gift from God, my precious son, was bestowed on me.

Three different times I begged the Lord to take it away. Each time he said, my grace is all you need. My power works best in weakness," so now I am glad to boast about my weaknesses," so that the power of Christ can work through me. That's why I take pleasure in my weaknesses, and the insults, hardships, persecution, and troubles that I suffer for Christ. For when I am weak, I am strong. (2 Corinthians 12:8–10)

I called the lady from the state one week later to update her on the outcome involving Daniel in the new program, and I informed her he did not want to attend. She gracefully accepted the decision that he was not going back. Daniel was no longer striving for that piece of the independence journey. He now wanted to live the life that he loved so much, and to be safe at home with his family. Although this book is about love is in the journey, it was not always smooth sailing, there were many rocky roads to travel and mountains to climb, for Daniel, me, and the family, because of all the challenges and obstacles we faced, but it was still done with so much love. The great news was my son survived, and so did my family. The group home journey was now officially over. Thanks be to God!

Very early the next morning, the king ran out of the lion's den. When he got there he called out in anguish, "Daniel, servant of the living God! Was your God who you serve so faithfully, able to rescue you from the lions? "Daniel answered "Long live the king! My God sent the angel to shut the lions mouths so they would not hurt me, for I have been found innocent in his sight and I have not wronged you, your majesty." (Daniel 6:19–22)

Chapter 21

Another New Beginning

WITH DANIEL NOW home for good, I enrolled him in a program in New Jersey. We called it the Friday night program. He took to this program very well, and was happy to be back home with his family. The man Mr. P who ran the program resided in New Jersey was also a teacher in New York City. He was always open to helping Daniel, and he was very well schooled on working with the disabled. He hired college students, and the program involved trips to many places. They supplied transportation for all their trips. The bus driver was a wonderful woman who worked for the township, and she still does to this very day. Daniel loved her. She was so kind and loving toward him; he couldn't have been happier. I continued on with my pending lawsuit from my home in New Jersey and went back to New York when I needed to converse with my attorney. This went on for long periods of time while Daniel was flourishing in New Jersey. I will say that the people I came across there were the best of the best. They were very aware of my son's hardships involving the agency in New York, and they were so attentive to him, which helped make the transition to New Jersey a good one. It was so much better than our previous experiences.

Evil Deeds

As time passed, I received another of my many calls from my attorney's secretary. This call was very different, to deliver some very bad news. Right away I asked if something had happened. She hesitated, so I assumed it was bad news about him being in the hospital. Well it *was* bad news, only it wasn't him being ill. She informed me he had a problem and would be leaving his law practice for some time. Surprised I asked how long, and she stated one year or more. She told me she would meet with me to let me know what had happened. At that moment my gut feeling was there was trouble ahead. I came to find out shortly after that my attorney was suspended from his law practice by the court. I also found out he was well aware of this legal issue he was dealing with way before he handed my lawsuit over to the agency in 2000. I was never informed that any of this was brewing. She told me every one of his clients would be informed by a certified letter that would be sent out to explain his leave of absence from the law firm.

By now my attorney had his own family law firm he was sharing with his father. I was informed letters were being written on his behalf by his family and colleagues to make it easier when the sentence was given to him. Here I was going through another tough time of my life, trying to put my family back together, and the one person who was supposed be there for Daniel and me and had taken an oath to uphold the law is now in trouble with the law himself! I sat there wondering what the hell I was going to do now He did not want anyone else to take over the case. Talk about feeling abandoned! What would I do? How would I go forward? Who could I go to? I had so many questions but so few answers. I thanked the secretary for being my eyes and ears for my case, and for guiding me on how to move forward. The suspension was in the newspaper, allowing the public to be aware he was falsifying applications with several other attorneys. He was siphoning funds from a mortgage company to keep his ailing law firm above water.

"For I, the Lord, love justice. I hate robbery and wrongdoing."
(Isaiah 61:8)

Such is the fate for all who are greedy for money; it robs them
of life. (Proverbs 1:19)

Of course there were people who believed my attorney received a harsh sentence because he was related to a woman of fame, while other attorneys received a slap on the wrist for the same crime. He only had a short time to put his affairs in order. He was found guilty of conspiracy and given a five-thousand-dollar fine. His sentence was a suspension of practice. It was nearly two years before he was able to return to his work.

"What should we do?" said the soldiers. John replied,
"Don't extort money or make false accusations. And be
content with your pay." (Luke 3:14)

Doing wrong leads to disgrace, and scandalous behavior
brings contempt. (Proverbs 18:3)

I was able to meet with my attorney before he went on suspension. Although he was not able to do any legal business, I met with him, and he informed me to go to his mentor, who was also an attorney. That mentor would guide me. He also told me his mentor would not personally be involved in the case; he did not want to bring anybody else on board. I asked him if I should look for another attorney, and he assured me it would be okay if he stayed on the case. I asked him how that could be done if he wasn't active and able to do the discovery. Over and over again, he reassured me that it could be done.

I was totally confused that I had a lawyer who himself was not upholding the law. Here I was dealing with another failure of this part of the system. I knew I had to do everything in my power to keep the case alive. He was not allowed to practice any kind of legal business while he was on suspension. He did tell me no one could stop us from meeting as friends, and so that was what I did for some time to exchange information on the case and audiotapes that the lawyer for the insurance company had requested for the discovery.

When the insurance lawyers became aware of his suspension, they put in for another dismissal of my seven causes of actions against the agency. After the papers were written up by the office to deny dismissal, we had to wait for the judge's decision. It had taken months and was a highly stressful waiting game. Then came another blow. My attorney informed me he had to let the eyes and ears of his office Mrs. R go. He told me he could not be a go-between for the two women in the office while he was on suspension. I could not believe this woman, who was the most loyal to him over the years, was let go. As time passed, I realized he kept the other worker on because he was well aware she knew all his secrets. They say keep your friends close, and keep your enemies closer. I could tell you he was certainly not loyal to the people he counseled.

Only fools say in their hearts, "There is no God." They are corrupt, and their actions are evil, not one of them does good. Terror will grip them, for God is with those who obey Him. The wicked frustrate the plans of the oppressed, but the Lord will protect his people. (Psalm 14:1, 5–6)

It is unfortunate, but we must come to the realization that the system can fail us many times. It is all around us everywhere we turn. But it is mostly the justice system that is out of touch. There are not enough laws today to protect our children. Where are the laws to protect us against the very people who are breaking their own oaths to protect the innocent? We have people of power— politicians, lawyers, congressman, senators, presidents, governors, coaches, teachers, priests, deacons, and many more—who commit acts of deceit. These people of power have no time to watch over our children because they have their own demons. We need to channel our valuable time to be voices for children who are suffering. Our children in every walk of life deserve to be our top priority. They are the most innocent of all, especially the disabled and the elderly. Never allow the system to beat you; otherwise we have failed our love ones.

Chapter 22

The Case

THE COURT CASE continued after my attorney returned to his practice. At this point, the case was in jeopardy and was severely hindered by the delay in discovery as a result of the suspension. The insurance attorneys for the agency were not given important documents in a timely matter, and the long-awaited decision needed to be given by the court to allow us to move on, or else the case could be dismissed. Through all this mayhem, the papers were filed, and the long-awaited decision by the court to have the case dismissed again came back in my son's favor. What came with all these obstacles was the work of my fraudulent attorney and an insurance attorney who was, to say the least, not to be trusted. One confiscated money illegally, and the other was the cash cow taking money from the insurance company. This system is broken and unfortunately will always be broken with corrupt and dishonest people in our society. It is up to us to keep these people at a distance while the honest ones fight the good fight.

Then he said to them, you like to appear righteous in public, but God knows your hearts, what this world honors is detestable in the sight of God. (Luke 16:15)

My depositions were done at four different times and approximately five hours each sitting. There was no other reason for this to have been so long and tedious, other than the insurance company for the agency was paying the attorney five hundred dollars an hour. On my last deposition, it finished up late, around 7:00 p.m. I needed to wait for a cab to go home. That left my attorney and the insurance attorney alone to talk in an office cubicle. I waited in the outer office and heard them speaking. My attorney was not aware I was still waiting for my cab. It was very disheartening to hear these two attorneys talking like old friends, chatting away about their business and personal lives. It was even harder to comprehend the insurance company attorney talking about the agency he was supposedly defending, stating they were running a mess of a show.

It had not taken too long for me to realize the insurance lawyer believed in what he said because it was not the agency he was defending, it was the insurance company who would pay out the money. This leaving the agency off the hook with no penalty for their horrific actions involving Daniel's care. The insurance attorney came out to my home in New Jersey to do the deposition on Daniel, which lasted approximately thirty minutes. It should have been an embarrassment for him to even put my son through that. I wondered if he had a moral compass.

Yes, what sorrow awaits you! For you are like hidden graves in a field, people walk over them without knowing the "corruption" they are stepping on. (Luke 11:44)

Tragedy Strikes

My husband was now retired from the police department. He was not the sit-at-home type, so he then started a job as an armed guard for Federal Express in New York City. He would call all of the time from the Brooklyn apartment that he still kept do to his job travels, and also not wanting to drive any longer. Having the family split up was taking an emotional toll on all of us. One Saturday I did not hear from him. My daughter and her biological father got in the car and drove to the apartment. She went up alone and opened the door. All of the lights were out, including the television that he always had on; my husband was a huge sports fan and always had on the game or the news. She walked into the bedroom and tripped over something while getting to the light. When she turned the light on, there he was, dead on the floor. I will never forget when I had to tell my son his stepfather had passed on. It turned out he had fallen and hit his head on the back frame of the bed. The medical examiner said the injury caused him to lose too much blood. The man Daniel knew for most of his life; the man who was there for every hospital stay; the man who took him to his favorite pet shop, the local video store, and on vacations; the man who supported him emotionally and financially was gone, and Daniel would never see him again. It was heart wrenching. Daniel took it very bad and would ask over and over, "Ma, why did he have to leave us?"

We had a small gathering of family and friends. It was July 3, 2006, and the police department did a very small but heartfelt arming of the guards. He also served in the navy, so I was handed his flag and sent off to pick up the pieces for my son, daughter, and grandchildren.

Chapter 23

Another Bombshell

DANIEL WAS NOW forty-two years old. It was June, almost a year to the day after my husband's passing that my son complained his back was bothering him. It wasn't a major concern at the time because he did have scoliosis, a slight curve of the spine due to his disability, and he wasn't getting any younger. We would joke that he was becoming an old man. Not too long before this, Daniel was checked out by the doctors for his regular checkup. He told me when he transferred from his wheelchair to his seat on the bus going to his Friday night program, he made his swing too fast and banged his back against the side of the seat near the window. I watched him all the following week, and he had no other complaints.

It was several months later my daughter went off to the nearby college, to attend evening classes for her RN degree. I stayed home and watched my four grandchildren and son. It was about 9:30 p.m. when she came home. Daniel wheeled into the bathroom to use his urinal as he always did. He came out with his urinal held high in the air, asking, "What is this?" I had to take a long look at what was inside to grasp the shock I was in. Inside was dark red urine. I felt like all the life drained out of me. I yelled to my daughter to hurry and take a look. She did right away and told me she was taking him to the emergency room. I remember I was overwhelmed with not knowing what was wrong; I was terrified of the unknown. After my daughter left, I poured myself a full glass of wine and placed it on the countertop. I wanted to pick up the glass and knock it down, but I didn't because I had four grandchildren to care for, and I needed to be alert. I remember that full glass staring back at me as the hours passed by.

It was approaching early morning, and I still had not heard a word from my daughter on Daniel's status. I was up all night pacing the floor while the children were asleep. I went over to the countertop where my full glass of wine stood. I picked it up, went over to the sink, and poured it down the drain. That was how I lived my life, always disciplining myself not to do anything that would hinder my family's well-being.

It was now 7:30 in the morning when my daughter and son arrived home. I was ecstatic to see them, and all I wanted to hear was that my son was okay. I was able to have time with my daughter alone so I could get some information on the ER visit. She said it was gallstones. I kept asking more questions, and she shrugged it off, saying he would be okay. The next day my ex-husband, who was now back in my daughter's life, was acting very secretive to me. Finally he told my daughter she should inform me that my son did not have gallstones; it was a mass on his left kidney. I cannot describe what went through my head at that time, but it was mayhem. I was informed of this information the next day because her father had told her I needed to know the truth, that she was not able to tell me the night before because she was terrified of my reaction.

Again I needed to discipline myself to keep my emotions together for the sake of my son, who had already sensed something was wrong but did not know what it was. He was kind and trusting, but he would always pick up on bad vibes. It was the hardest thing I ever had to do, keeping all these different emotions inside me without screaming. I set up an appointment with the doctor where I had taken my son for his physicals. The doctor went over his test results and informed me about the mass on his left kidney; he gave me the name and address of a specialist nearby. I went home and set up an appointment. I went with my daughter and son to the urologist and was told the kidney needed to be removed. I had to make a fast exit from his office, leaving my daughter and son there so my son could not see or feel my terror. After I pulled myself together, the doctor informed me my son had a very large tumor that had overtaken his left kidney. He also informed me although it was cancerous, once removed Daniel would not need chemo or radiation.

While listening to all this information, I felt like I was hearing it in a different language. I could not comprehend all that was being thrown at me in that moment. I needed to make another appointment to a doctor at a nearby hospital where I lived, to have a sit down on what options my son had. The doctor stated to me, as the previous doctor had, that the kidney needed to come out right away. He set up other tests to make sure the cancer had not spread. The results were in, and I was told everything else was clear.

I looked at my son, who was not capable of understanding the full impact of what was happening to him and was heartbroken. I had to make decisions that would affect his life. My daughter and I had full power of attorney to be able to enforce any of these decisions involving Daniel's healthcare. By now he was aware that something was going on. The first thing he asked was whether he had cancer. My son loved to watch TV, and many times he came across commercials on cancer. That was something he always talked about and showed such concern for the topic. I tried with every bit of my being to stay in control, and I reassured him he did not have cancer, but we needed to have his kidney checked so he would be able to continue living a good quality of life. My son trusted me with his life and never doubted for a moment I would do everything I could to make him better. I could not believe with all he had already endured in his life, it would end up with him being diagnosed with cancer. When Daniel came to permanently live back home with his family, he went on to be the picture of health and was strong like a bull. I would look at him and think, *This cannot be happening to my son. Why?* All this adversity in his life, and now we were going to face another battle to survive.

> *Dear brothers and sisters,*when troubles come your way, consider it an opportunity for great joy. For you know that when your faith is tested, your endurance has a chance to grow. So let it grow, for when your endurance is fully developed, you will be perfect and complete, needing nothing. (James 1:2-3-4)*

After our consultation with the doctor, we began the preparation of setting up his surgery. I would say over and over in my mind, *Why? Why? Why?* It never ended. My son still remained the happy person he always was. My daughter and I did research on the surgeon, and there was nothing negative to be said about him, so it was a go. All the needed tests were done. We conferred with the necessary doctors to clear the surgery. My daughter and son then went for the final pre-op visit. The doctor sat my daughter down in his office and told her he was not comfortable doing the surgery because he did not do many of them. He recommended we find a doctor who did this kind of surgery on a daily basis. She came home very upset that the doctor had not voiced his concerns sooner. We now had to start the process over of finding another doctor. I needed to take a few days to do some research and seek another opinion. This was a very big surgery, and I needed to do everything I could to do the best for my son. My daughter also did research and found a doctor associated with a very well-known hospital in New York City. She went to the city with Daniel and her father to meet with the doctor and go through his tests and records. I was too distraught to go and did not want my anxiety to upset Daniel. We were starting the process all over again. We had already lost a month's time planning the surgery in New Jersey. My daughter was extremely upset because all of Daniel's tests showed the cancer was confined to his kidney, and we wanted to keep it that way. Waiting for the surgery would only give the cancer a chance to spread. Daniel at this time was not experiencing symptoms of the cancer, except for an occasional pain in his back.

I valued my daughter's opinion on the visit with the doctor. She was my right hand in all aspects of Daniel's caretaking and she believed this was the doctor to do the surgery. We informed the urologist in New Jersey who was originally supposed to perform the surgery that we had found a surgeon in New York. He believed my decision was right, and although the surgery could be done in the hospital where he was practicing, he thought that it was better to have the surgery done in a hospital that performed this surgery on a regular basis. I respected his honesty and his bowing out gracefully but I like my daughter believed he should had done it sooner. I personally believe he was relieved I had made the right decision and so was I. We had multiple appointments to again prepare Daniel for surgery because they wanted their own testing done. After another month, we were finally ready. We assured Daniel the surgery needed to be done to keep him healthy as always, he trusted us. I will never forget when he asked, for the second time "Ma do I have cancer, am I going to die?" I told him no it was just a problem with his kidney. My daughter and I felt it best not to stress him out and to take the worry on ourselves. But that still did not take away his inner fears and anxiety. .

Chapter 24

𝒜 Rollercoaster of Emotions

TODAY SEPTEMBER 3, I prepared to take my son to the NYU Hospital in New York to set up the surgery. I felt like I was dying inside. Daniel was going to sit in the front seat as always. He entered the car with no questions asked because he trusted me with every fiber of his being. My ex-husband, Daniel and I were now settled in the car. It was a beautiful day. As I looked around everything seemed so tranquil. I thought *Why is this happening?* Then the car pulled away, and I wanted to jump out and run, but I sat there silently. We had to ride through our old neighborhood in Brooklyn to get to the hospital, and that made Daniel happy. He sat quietly as I tried to make some small talk but not babble too much; I did not want my anxiety to fall upon him.

We finally reached the hospital, went inside and entered this enormous lobby. This was the first time we had ever been there, and I prayed it would be our last. We had to go to the front desk and give information on Daniel's medical cards, while he sat patiently as always. After that, we proceeded to get on the elevator and go up to his room. It was then, when I wheeled my son into the room, that the full impact of the reality hit me hard. *Oh, God, why my boy?*

Daniel was now admitted into the hospital and the doctors wanted additional testing. He had to go through MRIs, chest X-rays, and more blood work, along with a consult with the anesthesiologist. Through all this, he was still a pillar of strength. He had no food intake and no liquids after 8:00 p.m. the night before. That was when he voiced his anger for the first time. He loved his Diet Pepsi, and taking that away pissed him off. The doctor and nurses came in and out of his room, and I hoped he would try to get some sleep and forget about how hungry and thirsty he was. We were both anxious, and it wasn't helping.

Early the next morning the doctor came into the room to inform me the surgery was canceled due to scheduling issues. I was surprised, somewhat relieved, and then disappointed because I wanted it over for my son. It was a big operation, and I was very aware that it was not going to be an easy one.

Now I was able to feed Daniel and give him his Diet Pepsi, knowing the same ritual had to be repeated the next evening. We were now scheduled for September 5. There was so much anticipation, not knowing if tomorrow's surgery was going to be canceled again. Around 6:00 a.m. the next morning, the doctors came in the room to say the surgery was a go. I was awake on and off most of the night from anticipation and a lot of anxiety. Daniel was awake, and I was very aware he was now anxious after two days of testing and waiting, along with doctors coming in and out of the room still, he never complained. I stayed by his side as we traveled down the long corridor and made several turns until we reached the elevator that had taken us to our destination, to prepare for surgery. I looked at my precious son lying down flat on the bed and looking so innocent and vulnerable. I wished to God it was me lying there and not him.

I love God's law with all my heart. But there is another power*within me that is at war with my mind. This power makes me a slave to the sin that is still within me. Oh, what a miserable person I am! Who will free me from this life that is dominated by sin and death? (Romans 7:22-23-24)

The anesthesiologist came out and introduced himself to my son. Daniel's sister was trying to joke around with him to lighten the mood. They were always teasing each other. She told him he was getting a tummy tuck, and she was jealous. The surgeon came over and made small talk. While we talked, I reassured my son everything was going to be okay. Daniel smiled—he always smiled. The doctor checked his stomach and marked the side where the surgery was going to be done. I joked with my son, saying, "X marks the spot!" Before they wheeled Daniel into the operating room, we were in a common area with other patients all waiting to be called into different operating rooms for surgery. The patients' relatives wanted to talk to different family members and converse about their loved ones. When Daniel was ready to go to the OR, I gave him a big kiss and a big hug, and I told him how much I loved him. He rolled off without a word. I stood there and felt like a heavy stone and my heart was broken as he went off to the operating room.

My daughter and I were informed to go upstairs to a waiting room. It seemed I was never going to get there. My ex-husband and his wife arrived, and we sat waiting. I had a hard time sitting, so I paced the floor for hours until I became extremely worried and anxious. When I was close to hitting the panic button, the surgeon's colleague came out to inform me everything was okay, but they could not remove the tumor laparoscopically as originally planned. They would have to remove it by going in and opening him up from side to side due to the close proximity of the main arteries that provided blood to the heart. Daniel's anatomy was a bit compromised due to his scoliosis. This meant a longer, more painful recovery, but it needed to be done.

More hours passed, and finally the doctor came out and informed me that the surgery was over. All in all, it took eight hours. I hugged the doctor tightly and told him I loved him for saving my son's life. He thanked me and reminded me we would be keeping a careful eye on my son because the tumor was cancerous. The entire left kidney was removed due to the size of the tumor. He also told us there was no spread of the cancer, and he was confident he got it all. I was so happy that it was over, time stood still for me at that moment.

I went to the recovery room and anxiously waited to see my son. After what seemed like forever, the nurse came out and informed us we could go in. I made a fast dash to see him, and he was awake and trying to sit up. I couldn't believe it! Then again, that was who he was: strong willed and tough as nails. I consoled him, and he wound up consoling me. He just had major surgery and was cut from one side to the other, but he was consoling me. Amazing!

After I spent some time with my son, I was told to wait for him to be sent to a room. He was transferred to a big room with six or seven other patients who were recovering from surgery, and that was where he was to spend the night. By the time he reached the room, he was very groggy. They gave him oxygen and a morphine drip, and they informed me I could press the morphine button when I believed he was in pain. Do to Daniels disability, I could not take the chance of leaving him alone. I sat next to his bed all night and made sure he was attended to. I also made sure his oxygen stayed on when it dropped under 100 percent. By morning I felt I was a patient myself tired and drained but with such a feeling of the world being lifted off my shoulders. I thanked God for pulling Daniel through this long surgery. Because of his disability, the lack of use of his right arm and a curvier of the spine, it was very challenging for the doctors to have him positioned just right during the surgery. He was sore all over from being in an awkward position for a long time. Now it was time for him to go to a private room. He was wide awake, and I continued to ask if he needed anything for pain. He said yes for the first few hours and then did not ask for it again. The doctors were amazed that after several days he hardly used any of the morphine drip.

Daniel had a seizure disorder as a result of the car accident, and he was on medication to control them. He could not take the pills by mouth, so they were giving him his medication through the IV.

One of the medications he was on did not come in IV form, but we were not informed of this prior to surgery. This caused a big change in his medication pattern. He started having multiple seizures, which he never had before, and he was violently vomiting piles of green liquid, a side effect of the anesthesia. They recommended to me that it would be a good idea for him to have a test to see how much brain activity he was having during his seizure episode. This would be done by placing many rubber tags with a gel attached to his head. I did not want to put him through that, especially because he was feeling sick and weak. The woman doctor kept asking me over and over. I finally agreed, and while my son sat in his chair, and the woman started the testing for the seizures. Halfway through, I told her to stop. It was a mistake to put him through this so soon after his surgery. The leads they attached to his scalp were uncomfortable, and the adhesive they used to attach them had a very strong odor. It made him nauseous, and he started vomiting. The woman doing the test apologized to me and said she was able to get enough activity just from the short time she was doing the test. I wiped my son's head with the washcloth to remove all the sticky glue that was in his hair. I felt guilty, dreadful, and angry that I had allowed the doctor to talk me into it. I found out later it was not even necessary. We knew he was having seizures, and we knew it was because of the mix-up with his medication. This is when I should have listened to my inner gut feelings about the test and said no.

Day five after the surgery, the doctor's assistant came in to the room to talk to me and remove his staples. Daniel did not flinch for a second. He sat there and allowed him to take them out.

It was now eleven days post-op, and I asked the surgeon when my son could return home. He thought it would be better if he was released so he was not subjected to any infection, so he agreed to discharge him. He was also aware that Daniel wanted to go home to be with the family. The nurse practitioner came in the next day to check out Daniel and go over the medications that he would need when he arrived home. She also set up a follow-up appointment for the surgeon in ten days. We were ready to leave and said our good-byes to the great, caring nurses. We were so grateful we were going home to another new beginning.

Daniel was given an antibiotic to go home with to prevent infection, called Cipro. He was now back to his doses of his own seizure medications by mouth, and he was tolerating it well. The day after Daniel arrived home, he started experiencing seizures at a high rate. They were nonstop. I realized right away that there was something wrong and that it was due to the change of the seizure medication given to him at the hospital. It was heart wrenching to see him go through this experience, especially due to the eight-hour surgery he had to endure to have his kidney removed. Thirteen days prior. Again we had to take him to another hospital in New Jersey close to our home to regulate his medications.

The hospital admitted Daniel, and he spent the next five days there while the doctors monitored his seizures. The doctor treating my son's seizures informed me the Cipro that he was given interacted with his seizure medications he was on, and it should never have been prescribed to him. I could not believe the hospital he just left in New York City would have made this mistake. My only concern now was to concentrate on having my son get better. It was three weeks of torture for him. I was exhausted and so angry that all of this was happening to him. Finally after the five-day hospital stay was over, we went back home again. Thank God, I was so grateful my son was alive and had survived another major setback.

It was a short time after surgery that we had a follow-up appointment with the surgeon. After a complete examination, he said that things were looking good. I asked the doctor if he could take a picture or two with my son. Daniel loved his pictures. The doctor was happy to comply. I told him how grateful I was for him to have pulled Daniel through a very difficult surgery and allowing my son to be here with me and the family.

After the exam, the doctor stated to me he was aware of the problem I had with Daniel's mix-up with the seizure medication and the Cipro. I told him I desperately just wanted to move on. He also suggested to me I could go to another doctor in New Jersey, and they could report back to him; it would make it easier on our travels. I declined because I just wanted to stay with him. I left the office and went down to the parking garage with Daniel and my daughter to return home. I was so happy to have heard good news about my son. On the ride home Daniel sat in the front seat and I sat in the back seat, telling him how pleased the Surgeon was with the visit. I know Daniel was very happy and relieved; he was smiling all the way home.

Chapter 25

Injustice

....

TO ADD TO this battle while Daniel was fighting his illness, my not-so-upstanding attorney, who had been suspended from 2001 to 2003, was back working on my case. My pending lawsuit was moving to trial the latter part of October, while Daniel was still recovering. My attorney was ready to hand out subpoenas to go to court when we received a notice from the insurance attorney that they had put in for another dismissal. I had to put myself back in the loop for the case to survive. My attorney knew I had no trust in him by now; he wanted my audio tapes to be transcribed so we could use them in court. He would not spend any of his own money to have them transcribed, so he suggested that my daughter have them done. I told him it was very time-consuming, and I could not take that much time away from my son. Besides, the fact is it is not legal to do one's own transcribing. I told him at this point I wanted to drop the case so I could focus on my son. He told me that there was too much time and money invested in the case to give up now. With much hesitation my daughter and I worked transcribing the tapes. It was our last hope to have the seven standing causes of actions against this agency remain as they had for the past eight years.

By now I realized the insurance company's attorney caught word that my son had kidney cancer, and just when all the subpoenas were going to be served, they believed this was the best time to strike. After all the papers were submitted by both sides, it was a matter of waiting. The decision came down from the judge that six causes of my actions were dismissed. I had a strong, gut-wrenching feeling this was going to be the outcome. There was so much deceit already going on behind closed doors.

I also noticed that under the sun there is evil in the courtroom. Yes, even the courts of law are corrupt! I said to myself, "In due season God will judge everyone, both good and bad for all their deeds." (Ecclesiastes 3:16–17)

How long, O Lord must I call for help? But you do not listen! "Violence is everywhere!" I cry, but you do not come to save. Must I forever see these evil deeds? Why must I watch all this misery? I see destruction and violence. I am surrounded by people who love to argue and fight. The law has become paralyzed, and there is no justice in the courts. The wicked far outnumber the righteous, so that justice has become perverted. (Habakkuk 1:2-3 -4)

The judge left me one cause of action and did not accept my non-legal audiotapes that my daughter and I had transcribed. The one cause of action that was left standing was my son's severe burns that he had received to his stomach. My attorney told me to reply to the judge in a written, sworn statement with my objections to the denial. I could no longer take any more time away from my son. It was now over one year since the surgery, and he was just coming around.

My court date was scheduled for October 2008, and this would be the end. I arrived at court in Brooklyn. I was only concentrating on my son's health. The insurance company's attorney was well aware that my son's health and safety was my first priority, and that's what he used as leverage to hit us when we were at our lowest. I remember so clearly, like it was yesterday. I sat at a big long desk with my son beside me. Directly in front of me was the court officer and a court stenographer. My so-called attorney and insurance attorney were conversing together. It put me back to being in my attorney's office when I was doing my depositions, and they were conversing in the office. I was wondering what deceitful strategy they were conversing about now. After about thirty minutes, the judge came out. I was already aware by now that six causes of my actions that had stood up for eight years were about to be over.

The judge introduced himself and wanted me to know although he was a good friend of my attorney's father, it would have no effect on the outcome of this case. I thought, *Yeah right! One big happy family.* Daniel sat patiently, and all I wanted to do was leave and go back home. The judge asked me if I would accept the one cause of action, the burns. He also advised me that if I did not accept the offer, he would have the jury come in, and did I want to subject my son to answering all these questions. Talk about using scare tactics to make a decision.

> *Those who convict the innocent by their false testimony will disappear. A similar fate awaits those who use trickery to pervert justice and who tells lies to destroy the innocent. (Isaiah) 29:21)*

The judge asked me if I wanted Daniel to go through any more stress. I answered of course not. Then he stated I should sue the state, because they were responsible.

> *You brood of snakes! How could evil men like you speak what is good and right? For what evil is in your heart determines what you say and I tell you this, you must give an account on Judgment day for, every idle word you speak. The words you say will either acquit you or condemn you." (Matthew 12:34–35-36-37)*

I had no intention of allowing my son to go through any more of these evil deeds, and they were aware of how much I loved him. They knew I would take his health and well-being over the case. I decided at that point to walk away and focus on Daniel's recovery. I believed the judge, my attorney, and the insurance company would all benefit monetarily from my walking away, and I was okay with that. I remember when the insurance attorney came over to shake my hand. I did not hesitate to put my hand out and exchange a few choice words. I told him it was never about the money; it was only about my son's safety. I went home not feeling defeated about losing the lawsuit. I felt defeated because my son had lost his father, his program, his lifelong friends, his dream of a group home independence journey and his kidney. Now he was fighting another battle for survival: to save his life.

Take no part in the worthless deeds of evil and darkness, instead expose them. It is shameful even to talk about the things that ungodly people do in secrets but their evil intentions will be exposed when the light shines on them. (Ephesians 5:11)

No one cares about being fair and honest. The people's law suits are based on lies. They can conceive evil deeds and then give birth to sin. (Isaiah 59:4)

Chapter 26

A Mother's Worst Nightmare

FOR ONE YEAR after Daniel's surgery, we watched him like a hawk. We took him for MRIs every three months. Then one of the MRI's showed quite a few little specs in his lung. I was frantic with worry. The doctor assured me his patients had them, and it was normal. He asked me if I had seen a pulmonary doctor. I said we never needed one before, so he recommended we have a more detailed look into Daniel's lungs. Her office was in the same building. I set up an appointment right away, and Daniel was taken to her office.

My daughter had taken Daniel along with her father on this doctor's visit. The doctor asked my daughter many questions, and the result was that my son was to have another MRI so she could take a look at another test that was done under her care. Daniel had his MRI a few days later, and the results was sent to the doctor. The phone rang. It was a colleague who worked with the pulmonary doctor. I used my tape machine to record our conversation. I wanted to record my conversation because I did not want to miss one word the doctor was going to tell me. I was so upset and nervous, and I didn't think I would be able to remember much of what he was saying.

The doctor picked up on my apprehension right away, and I was freaking out. He asked me why I was so upset, and I explained it was the waiting on the MRI results. He said the scan showed multiple tiny little spots, and the team looked at the scans very closely and assured me everything was okay. I told him about my concerns, and I didn't understand why all these spots were showing up. His answer to me was the MRI report always covered every little detail, and that was why the reports showed these issues. He also told me sometimes it was complicated for someone like me to read. He said to me the doctors doing the MRI scans needed to cover their backs. Whenever Daniel had MRIs or CAT scans I always insisted that they send the reports to me, and they complied. Many times when I read the reports, it was hard for me to understand what was in them, but I was able to make some sense of it. I hung up the phone from the doctor feeling relieved.

Three months later, it was time for another MRI. I received a call from the doctor's office, the results were in. My daughter called her office immediately and was told the cancer had spread to his lungs and was no longer treatable. The same woman doctor who had originally read the scans and had her colleague tell me not to worry, was now on the phone telling my daughter that the cancer had spread, and there was nothing they could do for him. I never felt truly confident that the tiny spot they had found on Daniel's lung when he was first diagnosed back in 2007 was not cancer, but through all their reassurances, I let myself believe it. After all, Daniel was under their care. I came to realize you are never too young or too old in this life to learn that the only person you can believe in and have trust in is God and yourself. You have to be your own doctor, lawyer, and politician, but most of all, you have to be your own advocate for your family. Sometimes you want to believe so badly that what you hear is the truth. They say the truth will set you free, but sometimes it can hold you hostage if you allow other people to guide your path.

Here was Daniel, one year after mourning his step dad's passing, being diagnosed with kidney cancer, and having his kidney removed. And taking over a full year to recover. Now we had the news that the cancer had spread. I was traumatized by this horrific news. I prayed inside my soul that this would go away. I would plead, *Please God, take these tumors out of him.* I would hold my pain inside and embrace my son in my arms, while he would tell me over and over again, "Don't worry, Ma Be happy. I'm okay." This beautiful soul with his godly spirit worried about me. Every day he would say, "Ma, I love you with all my heart and soul. Take me everywhere you go."

I love the Lord because he hears my voice and prayers of mercy. Because he bends down to listen, I will pray as long as I have breath! (Psalm 116:1,2)

I decided to seek another doctor in New Jersey, near where Daniel and I were residing. This was to make the trips easier for him to travel, and I was not happy with the pulmonary doctor in New York. Although Daniel was not experiencing any symptoms, the cancer was in his lungs now, and I advised his doctor in New York of my plans to change. I was informed by the surgeon who removed Daniel's kidney that if the tumor was caught earlier, it might not have spread and the very small cancer cell that had escaped from his kidney before his surgery was from the growth of the tumor, although there was no symptoms. It traveled up through the vena cava vein into my son's lung. The doctor my daughter found and did research on was located in New Jersey at a very well-known hospital. I begged him to help my boy and give him something to stop the spread of the cancer. Daniel was started on an oral chemo. In the beginning he tolerated it very well. After the treatment was complete, the follow-up MRI showed the cancer was still spreading. He then tried another oral chemo. Little by little, my strong and gentle giant became sicker and sicker. He could not eat. He had sores in his mouth. He lost interest in all the things he loved in life: Christmas, his video tapes, DVDs, watching TV comedy shows, his animal book collections, collecting telephones, being with his pets (especially his cat Nyla), his Friday night fun program, and his family and friends. The next

MRI showed the cancer had now spread to his liver. Although the doctor had a good bedside manner when he was treating Daniel, I was looking for a Dr. Hope. I had been through a life-and-death experience with Daniel in 1968, and I knew that without hope, you have nothing.

After the second oral chemo did not work, they decided to try Daniel intravenously on Vasten for three weeks, Monday to Friday, followed by two weeks off. Daniel tolerated it as well as could be expected, and I prayed that the third time would be the charm. I remember clearly when I went to one of his chemotherapy treatments. I bought an article I received in the mail from another local hospital that dealt with cancer patients in New Jersey. It was about a woman who had no hope of survival for her cancer, and then she received a trial treatment that put her in remission. When the doctor came to see my son on one of his chemo treatments, I showed him the article and tried reading it to him. He would not even acknowledge my being hopeful. The feeling I had when he walked out of the room was being so let down and overwhelmed. I needed him to say there was always hope, but I did not hear those words. When he left my son after the treatment, I experienced all different kinds of emotions. I had an overwhelming feeling of defeat sadness and despair. I could not lose hope—that would be Daniel's downfall.

Where then is my hope? Can anyone find it? No, my hope will go down with me to the grave, we will rest together in the dust!" (Job 17:15)

Chapter 27

Holding on to Hope

LOOKING BACK NOW, I know that I was very angry that day because I wanted so badly to have the doctor confirm my feelings of hope. I thought that was what being a doctor was all about. No matter what happens, never give up—but how do you have it if no one gives it to you? I was so sad and disillusioned by being unable to feel that from him. I looked at my son and kept going over what I could have done differently to have found this tumor growing inside my boy's body. Daniel trusted me with his life. Now I look back to when I had taken Daniel to his neurologist for his seizure disorder at our local hospital. I mentioned to the doctor that Daniel's urine was always slightly orange, and he told me it was the seizures medication. This visit would normally be every three to six months, depending on his seizure activity.

Daniel had a physical every year, which included a urine analysis and blood work. According to the doctors, the results never showed up any blood in his urine. I could not understand how this was possible; it did not make sense. The one thing he did not have was an MRI or CAT scan that would have shown the tumor in its early stages. Even the doctor who operated on my son's kidney stated to me if a MRI or CAT scan had been ordered earlier by the doctors treating my son, his chances of survival would've been much higher.

One of the most powerful medicines in the world is your voice. If you do not use your voice when it comes to your loved ones and advocate for them, then their voice dies.

When Daniel was done with his chemo, I made the decision to not give him anymore, because he was so ill and weak. His body had already endured more than he could tolerate. I wanted to let him build up his strength again and allow him to eat—something he loved to do. During one of the doctor visits, the doctor entered the room that I was in with my daughter and was accompanied by another physician. He asked me if I thought he was doing the best he could for my son. I answered yes, because I believed he had given Daniel medication that he believed was the best for him at that time. But spiritually, I was not receiving any support from him; I was not feeling the hope I needed, and it was now what I needed more than ever. He informed me that there was nothing more they could do for my son. After asking several more questions, I made a major mistake by asking him how much time he thought Daniel had. He stated two months. I was devastated. I sat with my daughter in that room and froze. After that, I wasn't hearing any more, my mind went completely blank.

> *This is my command—be strong and courageous! Do not be afraid or discouraged. For the Lord God is with you everywhere you go. (Joshua 1:9)*

I informed the doctor I was going to take Daniel to a well-known cancer hospital in New York City. He told me this hospital could be another source of help for my son because it was their specialty, and they had research trial study medications available to them that other hospitals did not have. I came to the conclusion very fast that I wanted to go to another hospital because I was looking for that Dr. Hope. All I wanted was to go the hope way.

> *Having hope will give you courage. You will be protected and rest in safety. (Job 11:18)*

I hooked up with a very caring oncologist, Dr K, in New York City who was comfortable to talk to, and Daniel liked him. I asked him if he could help my son, and after examining all his records, he said yes. He also spent time talking to Daniel about many different things. I explained to the doctor that my daughter and I had medical power of attorney, and the decisions I was making concerning his treatment was destroying me inside—the pain, guilt, anger, and all the whys. Why did Daniel have cancer? Why did I not find the cancer sooner? Why was I given such a gift but could not save him? Why couldn't this cancer be inside me?

The doctor wanted to put Daniel on a higher dose of the oral chemo than he was taken before. I was very concerned about that, but he said that many of his patients tolerated it very well, and he would watch Daniel closely. After a while of taking the pill, it was making Daniel very sick again. We had more MRIs and doctor visits. Daniel developed a nagging cough that was nonstop. I was due for another appointment in New York City to see Dr. K, but I had to cancel because he was too sick to travel. I had a doctor who was recommended by my daughter's friend who made house visits. I called for an appointment and spoke to the service. I explained that Daniel had a very bad cough and needed to have an X-ray of his lungs. The woman on the phone told me she would give all this information to the doctor before the appointment. I was told he could order an X-ray that could be done in the home. The doctor came and examined Daniel. He did not arrange for an X-ray. Instead, he recommended Mucinex to dry up the mucus Daniel had in his lungs. He also recommended that Daniel take laxatives, because he wasn't able to go to the bathroom for several days.

A few days later, Daniel was coughing up so much mucus that I put my son in my car and drove him a few blocks to my general practitioner. Daniel had a hard time getting in and out of the car. When I arrived, I went inside the office, and Daniel's coughing was nonstop. The doctor looked at my son and told me to get him to the emergency room ASAP. My daughter was just coming home from nursing school. We had to rush right out to the hospital.

After Daniel was checked out by the doctors in the ER and had X-rays taken, the doctor informed me he had pneumonia and was very dehydrated. He needed many infusions. The doctor took all my information and then informed the oncologist who had previously treated my son of his status. I told them I could not bring Daniel to the New York hospital because of him being so sick. After all this information was given to the doctor, I was informed that my son would have to stay in the hospital because it would be much safer for him.

My daughter and I stayed in the ER, which seemed like forever. Daniel was finally admitted into a room after several hours. The hospital had a lot of chaos going on because the flu was going around. Daniel was sharing a room with a very lovely man. He was an elderly man who was being treated for numerous medical conditions. He also had a heart condition, and he had around fourteen stents inserted. Over the next few days, his family came to visit him and spend quite a few hours with him, keeping up his spirits. I found him to be such a kind man, and I enjoyed talking to him when his family went home. He also spoke very highly of his family members; I could see that he really loved them. The roommate required the medical staff to come in and out frequently, in order to provide care. I would sit in the chair next to my son's bed and listen to them talking. One couldn't help listening because the beds were so close together.

One morning when the food tray came in, Daniel's roommate was in the bed trying to butter his toast. The tray fell on the floor. I ran over, picked up the tray, and told him not to worry because I would take care of it. I went outside to the nurse's station to ask them to send another tray because he dropped the one he had. Nobody ever came back, so I went to the nurse's station again and demanded that they get him another tray of food. After a while, another tray came up. I went over to his bed and helped him butter his toast and do anything else he needed. He thanked me and stated he was sorry to be a bother. I told him it was absolutely no bother at all.

It was early afternoon when a nurse came in and started asking the nice man several questions. I could see that he was getting a little bit agitated. She told him in a harsh voice he had to get up. "You are not allowed to stay in bed. You have to get up and move around." My son and I did not believe he was strong enough to get up considering his medical condition. That didn't stop the nurse from calling another nurse to get him out of the bed. After they stood him up on the floor, he collapsed. After that, it was mayhem. Many doctors and nurses rushed in the room, trying to get him off the floor. The doctor came in, and I could hear him yelling at the nurse, telling her he was not supposed to get out of bed. While all this was going on, my son and I were behind the curtain listening to all this chaos.

I could not leave the room. They blocked us in with all these different machines, so Daniel and I had to sit there and listen to all that was going on. Shortly after that, he passed away. My son and I were distraught. The elderly man stayed in the room for a number of hours, until the family came; each one sat and spent time with their father. One of the daughters approached me and asked if I knew anything about what was going on. As heart wrenching as it was for me, I could not bring myself to say anything. His daughter asked me if he said anything to me, and I replied, "All your father did was talk about how wonderful his family was." It was a very bad experience to have to go through with my son so sick, and I didn't want to add any more misery to the family. I was sickened by the way the poor man had been treated. I just wanted to get my son the hell out of there. I realized there was nothing I could do to save the man, but I did not want to give the family more heartache than they were already experiencing. He would have eventually passed from his medical issues, but I believe his death was a result of the nurse taking him out of bed against the doctor's orders.

Chapter 28

What Happened to Compassion?

....

FIVE DAYS PASSED, and we had no visit from Daniel's former oncologist. I was shaken and quite hurt by it. At the same time, I was angered but not totally shocked due to the lack of compassion on his part for not being my son's Dr. Hope. This was the beginning of November 2010, and we went home. Daniel was still so sick that by Thanksgiving he couldn't eat. He was a shell of what he used to be and had lost so much weight. All his medications were now stopped, with the exception of his seizure medication.

It was Christmas, Daniel's favorite holiday. He loved everything about it. We always made such a big deal of it because he still believed in Santa Claus. Although he still didn't feel well, he woke up and opened up all of his gifts with his family, who meant everything to him. As the days passed, he started coughing again and complaining of his back hurting. He was coughing up so much mucus. I made the decision to not take him to the New York hospital for the second time. I decided to take Daniel to the Doctor Oncologist office in New Jersey the one who treated the woman from the article I came across. I wanted to talk to the doctor to see what he had to offer my son. Unfortunately, the woman who was on a trial medication was not suitable for my son. He told me Daniel was not a candidate for treatment. He was a very kind doctor and was very candid with me. He told me after he had viewed Daniel's X-rays that once the liver was completely infected with these tumors, Daniel would go to sleep, and I would have to make the decision for what would be best for him. He said that Daniel would not wake up again.

Turn to me and have mercy, for I am alone and in deep distress. My problems go from bad to worse. OH, save me from them all! Feel my pain and see my trouble, Forgive all my sins. (Psalm 25:16-17-18)

Till this very day I continue to carry the pain, remembering the words he spoke to me. I found it so hard to believe my once strong boy who loved life would leave me. The doctor stated to me that when the time came, I would know how to make the right decision. I didn't fully understand what he meant. Unfortunately I would in time.

It was now New Year's Eve, and Daniel was complaining his back hurt. Laura and I took him to the emergency room at the hospital that was in the article because she thought maybe he' pulled a muscle while we were transferring him; he needed our help getting in and out of bed at this point.

It was the worst experience I have ever had in all the years of Daniel's treatment and of all the hospitals we went to, which were many. The few doctors I came in contact with were extremely rude. Daniel was given doses of medication too close to each other that needed Narcan, a reversible injection to get him out of a near coma state. It was hell. My son had to suffer again from another medical mistake. His X-ray showed his left lung was completely filled with fluid, and there was no doctor on staff to call to remove the fluid. I was screaming inside, *Why? This can't be happening to my son.* Still, he never complained.

I was told the hospital was understaffed because of the holiday. I kept thinking, *what the hell do I care about the holiday?* Were all patients in need supposed to have their illnesses put on hold because of the staff being on holiday? I said, "Screw the professionals out there." I felt so alienated to have my son again being in harm's way. When would it stop? My daughter was training to be an RN, and I pushed her to do it because her family came from a long line of nurses. I wanted her to do it to help others, like she always helped her brother. I was so angry with the treatment my son had that I wanted him out of there. I wanted her to quit nursing school at that moment, and then I realized she needed to stay because the sick needed compassionate, caring nurses like my daughter to care for them. God wanted her to do just what she was doing. That was her calling.

I told the nurse my son was in distress and needed to have the fluid removed from his lung. I told her if something wasn't done, I was going to raise hell. Shortly after that, the doctor on call informed me that a doctor was coming in to do the procedure. The interventional radiologist came in. My daughter and her father went down with Daniel to the room, where the procedure was to be done. Not an hour went by before my daughter came back into the room, and I asked her what was happening? The look that was on her face was indescribable. Right away I knew something had gone wrong. My daughter wouldn't allow the doctor to do it. She informed me that the interventional radiologist who was supposed to perform the procedure stated to her, while my son was in the room and wide awake, "I was called in for this? You have a choice. You can wait until next week, when we are fully staffed, or you can do it now, and he could die on the table. Either way, he is going to die anyway."

Even though Daniel was suffering, my daughter would not allow this kind of doctor to treat her brother. For her to do something like that, I knew that she did not want that doctor to put his hands on him. I immediately went to the phone to have Daniel transferred from where he was to the hospital in New York City. I believed that they were going to do everything to help me. I know they heard the pain in my voice with what my son was going through, and they would give Daniel the help he so desperately needed. Sometimes it is hard for other people to feel what you are going through when your family member is hurting, but the nurse I was talking to about Daniel and my situation truly felt my pain.

It was the day after New Year's, and the staff were still on holiday mode, but that did not stop my relentless voice from being heard. As I was waiting for the paperwork, a few nurses were very concerned. They even asked me to call them and give them an update on how my son was doing after we leave the hospital. While waiting, I walked up to the desk to where the attending physician was standing, and I asked him if he heard anything on my son's paperwork being put together so we could move on. The doctor stated to me, "Do you know who I am?" I told him, "I don't care who you are." He stated "It is not his job to do paperwork." I replied, "I don't give a damn what your job is. I want the paperwork done now." I went on to say a few choice words, and then I walked away.

Finally by late afternoon the paperwork came through, and that was my New Year's celebration: for Daniel, my daughter, and I to be able to leave this horrible situation. We needed to get him transferred so he could have the procedure to drain the fluid from his lungs. My daughter went through much guilt because she recommended we go there, but I assured her that I made the decision based on the article I read and the doctor I talked to. By no means did I blame the doctor who was affiliated with that hospital, because he had no involvement concerning my son's personal care. It was the few doctors and uncaring nurses who were to blame.

Chapter 29

Hope Finally Arrived

TRANSPORT FINALLY ARRIVED, Daniel was so happy to leave. It was such a frigid night on January 2, 2010, when the two EMS team members came up to his room. It was a man and a woman, and they handled my son with kid gloves. They made sure he was as comfortable and as warm as he could be, it took a short time to secure him in the stretcher. When I was walking out the door of the hospital, it felt like my son and I was being let out of a jail cell. There are truly no words that could describe what a person is going through while watching a loved one suffering. It's hell and back and back to hell again.

> *We proudly tell God's other churches about your endurance and faithfulness in all the persecutions and hardships you are suffering. And God will use this persecution to show his justice and to make you worthy of his kingdom, for which you are suffering. In his justice he will pay back those who persecute you. (2 Thessalonians 1:4-6)*

The ride to the hospital was quite bumpy due to the potholes from the winter weather. The supervisor let the woman drive for the first time, from New Jersey to New York City. I stated to the supervisor, "Will Daniel and I need another ambulance, given that we're being driven by someone you're training?" We laughed, and actually she was a very good driver. Daniel would add, "Hey, driver, are you trying to kill me?" He had such a great sense of humor, and no matter what trials and challenges he endured, he did it with such dignity. Daniel did not get his strength from me—I got my strength from him. He was my hero, my knight in shining armor, my prince. I had such admiration for him. Finally we reached our New York City hospital destination. The city was quite chaotic. When we were finally brought inside, I thanked the both EMS team member's for their commitment in helping the sick and comforting them, Daniel and I then said our good-bye's and thanked them for their kindness.

Daniel and I waited downstairs for a short period of time. I was very happy that he was being taken care of so soon considering there were so many people lined up downstairs. It was now January 3, and Daniel and I were in his room. I thought, *How did my son's journey wind up like this?* With all the roads we traveled together, and with every challenge and obstacle we had come up against, we had always prevailed. What were we doing here? We now had to face this monster inside him and try to stop it from breaking his beautiful spirit. I prayed, *Please, God, help my boy. Don't take him away. I love him so much. Please help me save him somehow, if the doctors and science cannot. I need you to go along with me. We cannot have traveled this long journey to have it end this way.*

A young doctor came into the room to evaluate my son, and he asked many questions and informed me that Daniel would get the best care to remove the fluid from his lung. On January 4 the doctors came in to Daniel's room and stated they were going to schedule my son for the procedure as soon as they had an opening. A short time later, I was informed by the doctor that it could be done at his bedside. I was not happy with that way, but at that time I felt we needed to do this as soon as possible to give Daniel relief, so I agreed after much hesitation. Shortly after that, the doctor came back for the third time to inform me that my son was going to be attended to the first thing in the morning in the operating room. I was so very relieved and thankful.

On January 5, Daniel went down for what I found out later was to be the first of several procedures of extracting the fluid from his lung. This was done by having a tube inserted in the back of his lung. I was also informed by the doctor earlier that Daniel's tumors were releasing watery mucus that continually filled up his lungs. Daniel was supposed to be put to sleep for the procedure, but after it was over, the doctors were quite amazed he went through it without general anesthesia. The doctor stated he took it like a champ. I was informed one liter of fluid was extracted from his lung, and they would have to wait a while before they went in for another fluid removal. They said it would be done in a day or two because they did not want the lung to collapse if too much was taken out at once. When the procedure was over, it felt like the whole world was lifted from my shoulders, because I knew my son would have relief.

On January 6 another procedure to drain fluid from Daniel's lung was done at his bedside by the nurse. He was to be released to go back home January 8, and I was to extract the fluid from his lungs when I arrived home with him. I was shown how to do this procedure by the nurse. I was so worried and concerned, and I was also afraid because Daniel was not eating. I worried about him starving. He was already showing bones through his skull, and his left arm, which had been strong like a bull, now looked like a long, thin branch.

Five days into Daniel's hospital stay, he was going home. The doctor wanted to have one more procedure done by the nurse to remove the fluid from his left lung. My daughter and I were in his room and next to his bed, and I held his hand, telling him that everything was going to be okay. The nurse was in the process of taking out the fluid from the tube when Daniel started to cough. My daughter told her to stop, and she said, "Don't worry. It is normal."

That was when everything went badly. Daniel was fighting for air, and everything became chaotic. They called a rapid response. Doctors and nurses rushed into the room, and I was pushed outside by the commotion. My daughter remained with her brother, and I waited for what seemed like forever.

An older doctor approached me; I believe he was the chief of staff. I had not seen this doctor before. The first thing I asked him was, "Is my son okay? Can I see him?" The doctor said yes. Daniel was now lying still with his eyes closed. I asked the doctor if my son was in a coma. He said no, but he had to put him out on a morphine drip because Daniel aspirated when he coughed, and because of this and his weak physical condition, the lungs were continually filling up with fluid.

After I stayed with Daniel for a while, the older doctor approached me to talk about having Daniel become a DNR (do not resuscitate). I was shocked beyond words. He explained it was in Daniel's best interests if I sign the consent form. I thought, *How could this be in my son's best interest?* I ran away from him and did not want to hear anything else. Shortly after, another doctor came to me to suggest Daniel be moved to another room so the family and I could be alone with him. I was very grateful for that. A short time later Daniel was moved to the far end of the corridor, where he continued to stay in a sleep state. I wanted him to wake up and needed to tell him how much I loved him and needed him so badly in my life.

On January 8 the older doctor approached me several times during the day to sign the DNR, and he explained what was going to happen if I did not. He explained he needed to be sedated because of his inability to breathe. I still could not comprehend what he was saying. Most of it was because of my fear of not wanting to deal with the truth. The doctor informed me if Daniel needed to be resuscitated if his heart stopped, it would be a very stressful act to revive him. I ran away again.

Later, the older doctor asked me if my daughter and I could come to the large conference room that was located in the center of the corridor. I realized that this was going to be something I did not want to hear. When we went into the office, the doctor wanted to put me on a three-way conference call to the doctor who had attended to my son's medical care and oncology for the past several months, after I left the hospital in New Jersey. The doctor made the call, but the connection would not go through for reasons unknown, so I wound up talking to the doctor one on one. To this very day, my mind cannot recall the conversation. I felt totally out of it, like I was in a cloud; I felt my body was somewhere else, and I had no saliva in my mouth. I felt my throat closing up on me. I was panicking and running around the office.

I personally believe the older doctor was in distress at watching me having a severe anxiety attack. I tried to swallow a glass of water and choked on it while trying to get it down. Whatever happened after that put me back to the reality that this was a very bad thing happening to my son. I then made the devastating decision to sign the DNR. I did not want my son to be pounced on and have his ribs broken; he suffered enough. The rest of the afternoon, family and friends, as well as doctors and nurses, came in and out of his room. My precious son was lying in the bed and looking very peaceful. I left the room for short periods to allow some family and friends to sit with him and talk.

I had been up for days and was totally wiped out when a young doctor that I had seen before on rounds came into the room just to talk about Daniel. I will call him Dr. Hope, to protect his true identity. At this time my daughter and I were the only ones in the room. He talked to me for a brief time about Daniel and who he was as a human being. He then stated that he loved my son's character. He spoke of the day he came into Daniel's room, and my son asked the doctor to help him pull up his pants. He laughed about that.

The doctor was exiting the room, when he put his hand on the door to open it and leave. He turned around and stated to me in a very quiet, calm voice, "I want you to know we are not given up on Daniel." After all the time, since my son had been diagnosed with the kidney cancer here he was the Dr. Hope that I was truly waiting for. I finally found him. I was so grateful for those few words—more grateful than anyone could ever imagine. Two Dr. Hopes were in the same hospital, and they both wanted to help my precious son when he was at his lowest point. I will never forget that through all his treatment and all the lows that my son reached, these two doctors were my Dr. Hope. They came at the most vulnerable time in Daniel's life, and knowing that there were people out there who really cared and wanted the best for their patients gave me back my hope. I painfully regret that I did not take my son to Sloan Kettering Medical Cancer Center in New York City at the very start of his treatment.

Instead, you must worship Christ as Lord of your life. And if someone asks about your Christian hope, always be ready to explain it. (1Peter 3:15)

As for me, my life has already been poured out as an offering to God. The time of my death is near. I have fought the good fight, I have finished the race and I have remained faithful. (2 Timothy 4:6-7)

It was now 2:00 a.m. in the morning on January 9, 2010. The last of the visitors had left. Laura, one of my son's best friends, and I were in the room with Daniel. There was a lounge chair next to my son's bed, and I wanted to rest for a short time because I had been awake for so many days. After I dozed off, I woke up to a very loud, sizzling noise. The TV in front of me on the wall had snow and then changed back to regular mode, because my daughter, who was sitting directly against the wall facing Daniel's bed, heard the loud noise and jumped up to change the channel. I was still groggy and sleep deprived, and I laid back down. My daughter went to her brother's side. She was aware that her brother, whom she loved with all of her heart, was now leaving this world to go to his new heavenly home, she told her brother to go to his best friend Herbie, who was waiting for him, and she said that she loved him very much. My eyes opened. Laura was standing up beside her brother's bed and looking over at me. She said, "Ma, he is gone."

> *"Don't let your hearts be troubled. Trust in God, and trust in me. There is more than enough room in my father's home. If this was not so, would I have told you that I am going to prepare a place for you? When everything is ready, I will come and get you, so that you will always be with me where I am. And now you know the way to where I am going."* (John 14:1-4)

Daniel passed on January 9, 2010, at 4:38 in the morning. Oh, God! I was in so much pain over the loss of my beautiful boy, who so wanted to live an independent life like every other good human being and thrive. From that time until 9:00 a.m., I was able to spend four hours and twenty-two minutes with my son. No nurses or doctors came into his room through the night. I had that precious time with my son because it was given to me by the grace of God.

> *And when he comes, he will open the eyes of the blind and unplug the ears of the deaf, the lame will leap like a deer and*

those who cannot speak will sing for joy! Springs will gush
forth in the wilderness, and streams will water the wasteland.
(Isaiah 35:5–6)

I called a close friend who owned a funeral home and made arrangements for my son to be picked up. I did not want him taken to the morgue. I wanted his body with me while his spirit went on to his new journey with God, his best friend, step-father, and his pets whom he had not seen for a very long time and missed so much.

When the new shift came to check on Daniel, that is when they were made aware he had passed on. All the doctors and nurses expressed how sorry they were for my loss. By now the funeral director came to my son's room, and I was left alone with my son for a few more precious minutes. The time came for us to leave. Daniel and I made the walk down the long hospital corridor. This was the final walk on our earthly journey. My Journey has not ended with Daniel's passing, he and I are a team. He moves me to continue on this journey of love.

David replied, "I fasted and wept while the child was alive,
for I said, perhaps the Lord will be gracious to me and let
the child live." But why should I fast when he is dead?
Can I bring him back again? I will go to him one day, but
he cannot return to me." (2 Samuel 12:22–23)

Missing You

Your heart that beat since the day you were born was the heart that ceased on that cold January morn.

I too passed on that day, but Dan, I could not cross over, for I needed to stay.

Your spirit left your beautiful soul. Oh, how I grieve that together we could not grow old.

I have unfinished work that needs to be done, and when it's over, we will meet again, my kind, gentle, loving son.

Love Forever, Ma

> *So you have sorrow now, but I will see you again, then you will rejoice and no one can rob you of that joy. At that time you won't need to ask me for anything. I tell you the truth, you will ask the father directly, and he will grant your request because you use my name. (John 16:22–23)*

> *"He will wipe away every tear from their eyes, and there will be no more death or sorrow or crying or pain. As these things are gone forever." (Revelation 21:4)*

Alone

I'm in a room with a thousand people and I still feel all alone.
I pray to God every day, please come and take me home.
Since my precious son passed on, life for me has long since gone.
The loneliness will stay with me, till the
day God comes to set me free!

Best Friend's Memorial Letter to Daniel

There is no way to describe Daniel in one sheet of paper, but I will try to do him some justice. I've known Daniel and his family since I was a little girl. Daniel was always happy, loving, and a natural-born comedian, and we all shared a bond. He had a great love of animals. His mother and sister would take him to the pet shop, and he would come home with a wide variety of animals, even ones that Mom and his sister didn't like so much. But despite them not always being in agreement with his pet of choice, they still supported it because it made him happy. He always knew the right things to say in fewer words than most people could express, and it always made a great impact on those closest to him and on everyone he met. Ever since we were kids, he would ask if I would be his girlfriend or wife. I told him no, but if I had half a brain, I would've said yes. Though had I, I would have had to share him because this was his way of expressing love to those who he had cared most. Daniel was very mature and had a unique way of looking at life because of his sensitivity. He always enjoyed the company of his closest friends and family, and he brought everyone closer. No matter how far apart we were or how long it had been, it was as if we'd never left. Daniel single-handedly kept Pepsi Co. in business as an avid lover of soda. He used to love the movie *Grease* as much as he loved Pepsi, but thank God he grew out of that. So long as he had a can of Pepsi and a good movie to watch, he was a happy camper. We are all very lucky. His mom, sister, and family, and all the people he loved, have God's greatest angel to watch over them.

Love Always,

Your best friend Carissa

The Medium

Shortly after Daniel's passing in 2010, my daughter's girlfriend told me about a medium; I will call her Medium M. The friend had gone to this medium in the past and wanted to make an appointment for me, but there was a two-year waiting list. As a skeptic, I did not put much into it but agreed to let her put me on the list. I was in so much grief and pain that I was numb with so many things going on around me.

Eight months since Daniel had passed, out of the blue I was taken aback by a phone call I received. It was the medium's secretary to confirm my appointment for October 28, 2010. I answered yes to confirm and did not ask why my appointment had been bumped up.

My best friend had passed away on October 11, 2010, nine months after Daniel. When I went to the funeral to pay my respects, I stood in front of the casket. I looked at her and thought how beautiful she looked, especially because she looked so sick ten months earlier at Daniel's wake. It was not the makeup; she was simply glowing and looked like an angel. We were best friends. I talked to her for a short time and quietly asked her to give Daniel a big hug for me when she met up with him. My son loved her, and she was family.

Two weeks after the funeral, it was time for me to have my reading at the medium's home. As my daughter was driving me from New Jersey to Staten Island for my appointment, she had a little difficulty finding the house. I took this to be a sign to go back home, and I asked her to turn around. I had such mixed emotions about going. She pulled over to calm me down and made a phone call to a friend to look up the right way to go. It turned out we were not far away from our destination. I was running late for my appointment, but the prior appointment before me went late, and it was my daughter's friend.

When I entered the house, the medium's husband greeted me. He appeared to be wearing oxygen; I found out later from the medium he had emphysema. He told me to sit down in the foyer on the bench, and she would be with me shortly because she was running late in her reading. The house was decorated inside and out with Halloween figurines. I felt like I was back in time. The house seemed old but very quaint with a lovely porch. It was a little creepy, but a good creepy, if you know what I mean.

My daughter's friend had waited two full years for her appointment. She came out of the reading visibly shaken. She was holding papers in her hand on which the medium had written. She showed me my son's name in large letters written across her page. The median told her, "Your friend's brother is very anxious and excited to see his mom, who is waiting outside." It turned out the secretary had called me for the appointment by mistake. It was supposed to be the other woman who worked with my daughter's friend at her job. This was God's intervention.

I went in and sat down. I had brought a picture of Daniel but had it face down on her table, and the reading began. I did not volunteer any information about my life, but from the very start she knew plenty about it. The first thing she said while writing on papers was that my son was excited to communicate with me. Then she paused and stated, "He is such a character." She stated he was with the cop, who was his step dad. He said congratulations to the nurse, his sister, who graduated four months after his passing.

The medium started to rub her legs and asked me if my son was in a wheelchair. I answered yes. She told me, "Well, not anymore he's not." She stated he was with his best friend, who passed away several years before him and missed him so much. Then she said they were both running and zooming all over the place. She was aware that my twin grandchildren were a boy and girl, age five; she stated their birthday was in June. She was on the mark with everything. She also knew about my older grandsons, who were experiencing a hard time because of their father's abandonment and the loss of Daniel.

She said Daniel kept repeating, "Ma please don't forget about God or be angry at him for taking me away." He said, "God already gave me forty-two more years with you than I was supposed to have."

She asked me, "What happened to Daniel forty-two years ago?" Followed by a short pause, she stated to me, "It was a car accident." She also told me his last several months before passing were very painful and hard for him, especially the last few hours when he heard us talking to him and he could not answer. She was on the mark.

There was so much more that she knew about Daniel that most people did not know. She knew the school he had attended and even what street it was on. What blew me away was when medium M stood up and put her arms around me. I was clueless as to why and asked her what she was doing. She told me she was giving me a hug back from Daniel—the one that I asked my best friend to give him at her funeral. There is so much more to say about that day, but I will keep that to myself. I will say I was in so much pain and grief, and God allowed me to have this one connection with my son. Before I went back home I made an appointment with the medium to go back in two years for another reading.

Faith is the confidence that what we hope for will actually happen; it gives us assurance about things we cannot see. (Hebrew 11:1)

My New Life

Last Jesus replied, the Kingdom of God can't be detected by visible signs! You won't be able to say, here he is! For the kingdom of God is already among you. (Luke 17:20)

I went home and started reading the Bible and taking Bible courses online. I soon connected back to the church. While reading the Holy Bible, I found out that God does not want anyone to go to mediums. He wants his children to believe and have faith in him, even when we cannot see him. I felt it was the ultimate test of my faith, and if I went, I would be disobeying God's wishes. Two years later, the appointment came up, and I gracefully declined. Although I passed up my next appointment, I am so grateful for my one-time connection to my son, and I will continue to wait for my signs from God.

I believe in God, but I also believed the medium was connected to me by God for the sole purpose of my being connected to my son. The medium was a tool God used to save me. When I was leaving the medium's home, she put her hand on my shoulder very gently and stated to me, "Remember, do not forget about God." After I went home, I spent many months trying to figure out how she knew so much about my son, especially because she never knew him or my family. After many months of trying to analyze the reading she gave me on my son, I came to the conclusion she was the real deal, and God gave me a special gift. I lost my beautiful son at age forty-five years old. It does not matter how old your child is or how he or she is taken from you. It's devastating. Parents are not supposed to lose their children. No words can ever describe the loss and emptiness you feel. I can only say that I am in a league of my own. Even when I try to feel others' pain and grief, it becomes too overwhelming. It is so very deep and painful and takes over your life.

When I was old enough, Mom would tell me I would hopefully never have to experience the loss of a child, as she had. She would tell me if I had children, it was a continuous worry from the cradle to the grave. Unknown to me back then, I would someday suffer the same horrific blow in my own life with the loss of my beautiful son. This was history repeating itself. What I believe I felt back then with Mom's pain and loss was nothing compared to the pain I was experiencing. I know now how she truly felt, and for that I am so sorry, Mom, for the loss of your son.

> *Then Jesus turned to his disciples and said, God bless you who are poor, for the kingdom of God is yours. God blesses you who are hungry now, for you will be satisfied. God bless you who weep now, for in due time you will laugh. (Luke 6:20–21)*

Conclusion

DANIEL FOUGHT GALLANTLY through his car accident in 1968, and he survived to go on and live a life he so loved. Through the years he faced so many challenges and obstacles that came up against him with such strength and determination. This allowed his spirit to flourish so he could continue on. Trials and adversity were a large part of him being the undefeated champ he was. He believed in survival no matter what he had to face ahead of him. My son was going to fight the fight regardless of his physical challenges, the group home journey that put him in harm's way, or his cancer diagnosis in 2007. The message is to never give up. This book's lesson is although it is very important to receive justice for my son, it is more important that it shows justice for the life he lived and loved. It was not all about the bad and the ugly, because there was so much good and beauty in his life that overshadowed the dark clouds.

Daniel was a special human being. He brought so much love and happiness to others. He loved people and was a true animal lover. He was my special gift from God, and I was given the highest honor to be a mother to this incredible human being with a beautiful spirit and soul. Daniel was a soldier who fought many battles and always won the war because he was so vigilant. Defeat is poison to the human body; it is brought on by dishonest people who are put in their power positions by being voted in. They can also be voted out. The same people who are there to protect our children can also use that power to destroy them. You must play a part in being your own politician, lawyer, doctor, and storyteller. Fight the fight to receive the justice your child and your family deserve. We must be the advocates and voices for all of our loved ones. There is nothing better than being your child's legacy.

There is so much pain I have endured every day in my heart since my precious son passed on. I miss his smile, his laughter, his strength, his courage, and most of all his love and zest for life. There is not a moment of the day that I do not carry him in my heart.

I will comfort you there in Jerusalem as a mother comforts her child. (Isaiah 66:13)

When it comes to a child's life and safety, what could be more important? I found out along my journey with my son that safety for our children is not the first priority to people of power in high positions. Do these people care for the lives of our loved ones? Not always. I found out because I was part of the process of experiencing that power over safety and money. If these group homes for the disabled were supplied with cameras for the safety of our consumers, I am very confident many of these horrific incidents could have been avoided. If the staff was aware the consumers were being watched, it would deter them from acting out, and if the abuser is caught, he or she could be held accountable. We are talking about lives here. All lives matter. Our consumers need to be protected from harm's way. Bad things happen behind closed doors.

Unfortunately sometime in life, we all need to depend on someone or something to help us. But this may not always turn out the way we want. We can turn to some really bad people, whether they are common, professional, or of power. They can do you more harm than good. You must be vigilant in everything you do, and everywhere you turn. Bottom line, be your own best friend and advocate. Never trust anyone one hundred percent with all your being. In time of need first trust your gut feeling.

We need family, friends, mentors, advocates, and even acquaintances to put their voices out there. We need to be the voices for those who cannot fight for themselves. We cannot tolerate anything other than to be the power of advocacy above all other power. Without all our voices, the disabled, our children and the elderly will be subjected to abuse—or they'll even die, as I have seen along my journey with my son in the system. At age seventy, I am doing what is right for families and their loved ones. It is never too late to make a difference. I do not have star status for my voice to be heard in a different forum, but I do have love and commitment and that is all I need.

While I was at the end of writing this book, I had been continuously struggling with thoughts of have I made my son proud. Then a revelation came to me. If I were to write this book a million times over, it could never express what an extraordinary human being Daniel was and the struggles he encountered in the system. I can only hope and pray this book brings awareness to the need to advocate for our loved ones.

> *If you try to hang on to your life, you will lose it. But if you give up your life for my sake, you will save it. And what do you benefit if you gain the whole world but lose your own soul? Is anything worth more than your soul? (Matthew 16: 25-26)*

Post Script

My son's biological father and I never did reunite, I consider myself blessed to have had this man in my life to have been able to share such a magical time. I will forever hold him close to my heart.

Although my ex-husband had his issues, he was not a monster by any means. He did come back into my daughter's and son's lives, and when Daniel became ill, he stepped up to the plate to help by going on many of the doctor visits with Laura and me. He also spent quality time with both of them. His wife jumped on board and put all of herself into being there for my son in every way possible before and after his illness, and I will be forever grateful for that. This is a woman who truly turned out to be a godsend to Daniel and the family. Daniel loved her, and she was his Mom #2. As the years passed by with much soul searching along my journey through church and scripture, I found that forgiveness and love are the most important parts of life.

I also need to clarify a very important part of Daniel's group home journey that involved the two staff members I brought over from NYC to Daniel's Brooklyn residence. Although they were both terminated from their job positions, in the years prior they spent with my son, they were loyal and caring or I would never had suggested they come over and oversee his care. Yes, they both made human errors by their actions but I do know in my heart they never intended to hurt him. Daniel truly loved them and so did my family. There were so many caring people in the organization who did the best job they could with the tools they had. They gave their time, commitment, and love to the consumers. It only takes a few bad apples to hinder many good ones. God bless all those caretakers who give their all to our children and the staff who cared for Daniel. Also a thank you to the secretary, Mrs. B. who was the core of the residence. She was a tool God sent to watch over my son.

But when you are praying, first forgive anyone you are holding a grudge against, so that your father in heaven will forgive your sins. (Mark 11:25)

"If you forgive those who sin against you, your heavenly father will forgive you. But if you refuse to forgive others, your father will not forgive your sins. (Matthew 6:14-15)

Final Scripture

These trials will show that your faith is genuine, it is being tested as fire tests and purifies gold- though your faith is far more precious than mere gold. So when your faith remains strong through many trials, it will bring you much praise and glory and honor on the day when Jesus Christ is revealed to the whole world. (1Peter1:7)

Printed in the United States
By Bookmasters